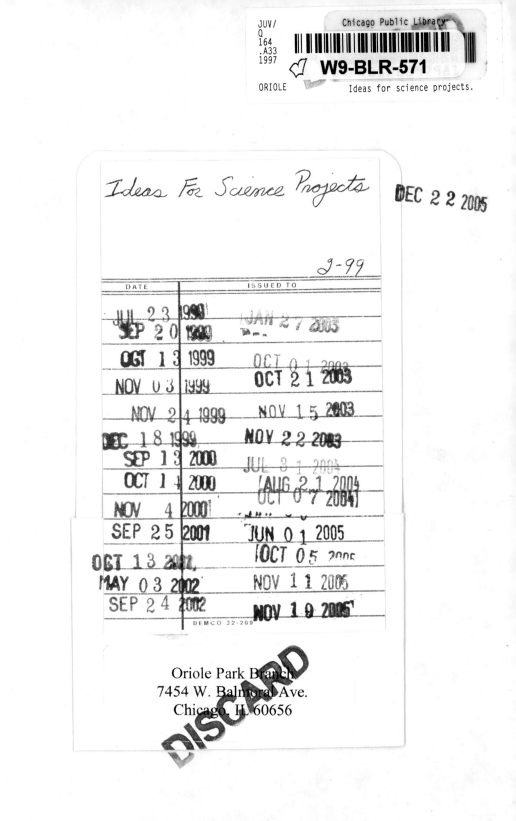

Ideas For Science Projects

DEC 2 2 2005

9-99

DATE	ISSUED TO
JUL 2 3 1999	JAN 2 7 2003
SEP 2 0 1999	
OCT 1 3 1999	OCT 0 1 2003
NOV 0 3 1999	OCT 2 1 2003
NOV 2 4 1999	NOV 1 5 2003
DEC 1 8 1999	NOV 2 2 2003
SEP 1 3 2000	JUL 3 1 2004
OCT 1 4 2000	AUG 2 1 2004
NOV 4 2000	OCT 0 7 2004
SEP 25 2001	JUN 0 1 2005
OCT 1 3 2001	OCT 0 5 2005
MAY 0 3 2002	NOV 1 1 2005
SEP 2 4 2002	NOV 1 9 2005

DEMCO 32-209

IDEAS FOR SCIENCE PROJECTS

Revised Edition

Richard Adams
and Robert Gardner

Experimental Science

Franklin Watts
A Division of Grolier Publishing
New York • London • Hong Kong • Sydney
Danbury, Connecticut

Note to readers: In most cases, measurements are given in both metric or English units. Wherever measurements are given in only one system, the units provided are the most appropriate for that particular situation.

Photographs ©: American Museum of Natural History: 18 (#210085); Fundamental Photos: 91 (Richard Megna), 59 (Paul Silverman); Photo Researchers: 89 (Barbara Burnes), 53 (Richard L. Carlton), 116 (Jack Dermid), 17 (Hermann Eisenbeiss), 111 (Phil Jude/SPL), 83 (John Kaprielian), 39 (Mount Wilson and Palomar Observatories), 133 (Charles J. Ott), 129 (Laurence Pringle); Photo Researchers: 50 (Arthur Tress).

Library of Congress Cataloging-in-Publication Data

Adams, Richard C. (Richard Crittenden)
  Ideas for science projects / Richard Adams and Robert Gardner. — Rev. Ed.
  p. cm. — (Experimental science)
  Rev. ed. of: Ideas for science projects / Robert Gardner. 1986.
  Includes bibliographical references and index.
  Summary: Introduces the scientific method through instructions for observations and experiments in biology, physics, astronomy, botany, psychology, and chemistry.
  ISBN 0-531-11347-7
  1. Science projects—Juvenile literature.   [1. Science projects.
2. Experiments.]   I. Gardner, Robert, 1929–   Ideas for science projects.   II. Title.
III. Series: Experimental science series book.
Q164.A33   1997
507'.8—dc21   97-3457
                                                                      CIP
                                                                      AC

CONTENTS

INTRODUCTION

Scientists solve problems by making careful observations, carrying out experiments, putting known information together in new ways, or a combination of all of these. Doing a science project will help you understand how a scientist works. You will formulate hypotheses, conduct experiments, make observations, try to draw conclusions based on evidence, and report your findings.

For most of the projects in this book, you'll find a number of questions you can answer by doing experiments. For example, the question "Does a dehumidifier really reduce the moisture in a house?" can be answered by measuring the humidity before and after a dehumidifier is turned on.

While doing the projects suggested in this book, you may discover new questions that you can answer through experiments you design yourself. By all means carry out these experiments—after checking with an adult to be sure they are safe. You're developing the kind of curiosity that characterizes a good scientist!

In his book *How to Do a Science Project*, David Webster writes, "Perhaps the hardest part of doing a science project is getting an idea to work on." It's reasonable to ask which brand of paper towel absorbs the most water. But it makes no sense to ask Bill Cosby's famous question, "Why is there air?" or "Why is there gravity?" because these questions simply have no answers.

The purpose of this book is to give you some ideas to work on. Some of the projects are simply questions designed to stimulate inquiry. Others contain fairly detailed instructions about how to proceed, but even these usually include additional questions that could lead to more individual inquiry. If you're new to the game of science, you might want to start with a project that's described in detail. After you've done some science, you may want to pursue more open-ended projects.

This book contains more projects than you could ever do, in a wide variety of topics. You may want to try projects from different chapters to find where your interests lie. Some people say, "I don't like biology," or "I don't like physics" without ever trying it. Once you get into a project, you may find it's a lot more interesting and challenging than you expected.

THE METHODS OF SCIENCE

You may have heard that science projects will teach you the scientific method. Despite what you've heard, no fixed method is followed in science. Each question must be explored in a unique manner. However, some principles are common to all modes of scientific inquiry. These include reference to previous research, use of the senses, trial and error, experimental controls, repetition, and experimental errors.

SAFETY FIRST

1. Maintain a serious attitude while conducting experiments. Fooling around can be dangerous to you and to others.

2. Read through the instructions carefully before beginning with any experiment described in this book. If you have questions, check with a knowledgeable adult before you start.

3. If you're designing an experiment of your own, check with a knowledgeable adult before you actually perform the experiment. There might be a flaw in your design that could cause an accident.

4. Wear protective goggles whenever you are doing chemical experiments—or any other experiments—that could damage your eyes.

5. Don't touch chemicals with your bare hands unless instructed to do so. *Always wash your hands after conducting experiments involving chemicals.*

6. Don't taste dry chemicals or solutions. Don't eat food while conducting experiments.

7. Don't inhale fumes released during a chemical reaction. Experiments involving poisonous or irritating gases should be done in a fume hood.

8. Keep flammable materials away from heat sources.

9. Keep your work area clean and organized. Make sure that nothing, such as gas or electricity, is left on when not in use.

10. Have safety equipment such as fire extinguishers, fire blankets, safety showers, and first-aid equipment available while you are experimenting. Know exactly where this equipment is.

11. Clean up chemical spills immediately. If you spill anything on your skin or clothing, rinse it off immediately with plenty of water, then report what happened to an adult.

12. Be careful about touching glass that has recently been heated; it looks the same as cool glass. Bathe any skin burns in cool water or apply ice.

A scientist generally begins research by consulting books and journals to learn what others have found about the topic in question. However, for most of the ideas suggested in this book, it would be better to proceed on your own so that you develop a sense of exploring what is unknown to you, even if the question has been answered by others. In a few cases, you are directed to some previous research to get you started.

Scientists use their senses—sight, hearing, touch, smell, and taste—to observe data related to their questions. They have also invented microscopes, telescopes, chemical tests, and various measuring devices to extend their senses.

In many cases, if an observed effect may be due to a variety of causes, a scientist will focus on one factor and then another in a trial-and-error fashion, trying to determine which one causes the observed effect.

Whenever possible, scientists use experimental controls; that is, they test the effect of a single variable at a time. For example, suppose you think temperature affects the rate at which water evaporates. You take two samples of water, exactly the same in every respect, except that one sample is warm and the other is cold. If the warm water evaporates faster, you've made your case. However, if the warm water was in a place where the wind was blowing, while the cold water was in an enclosed box, you could not be sure whether the increased evaporation was due to temperature or wind.

Repetition is vital to science. Experimental results must be repeatable. If your data do not agree with the data of someone else doing the same experiment, scientists will not accept your conclusions, because they're based on data that can't be confirmed.

No matter how careful you are, every experiment contains errors. You can measure something with a ruler to no better than 0.1 millimeter (mm); the temperatures you measure are no more accurate than the thermometers you use to measure them; the times you obtain depend on the watch or stopwatch you use. Observations depend on the number of times you see one thing as opposed to something else. You might see 1,000 robins flying south and decide that the robins were migrating. Then on the next day, you see 800 robins flying south and 200 flying north. Now all you can say is that 90 percent of the robins seem to be flying south.

Experimental errors are relative. To an astronomer, a difference of a light-year from one measurement to another may be insignificant, but to an atomic physicist a difference of 10^{-10} meters in two measurements may destroy a theory.

THE NOTEBOOK

As you start a project, keep a notebook. A spiral book that includes graph paper will allow you to make graphs of your data or scaled drawings of experimental equipment or designs. Record what you do, the data you collect, and the tentative conclusions you make. Be as thorough as possible. You may think you'll remember an observation, but if you've forgotten it a week later, you'll have to repeat the experiment. And if the experiment is based on something you saw in nature, that may not be possible.

THE PLAN

Begin your project by writing a statement of the problem you are investigating. This is usually a question. Then write a plan that you intend to follow to answer the question. Your plan might include equipment you'll need, drawings, and a time schedule. Recognize that your plan may change. All scientists expect problems. Things seldom work out as planned; if they did, science would be far less challenging than it is. There will be breakage, leaks, or seeds that fail to germinate; there will be mistakes, data that make no sense, and failure to control some unexpected variable. Don't be concerned if your project doesn't lead to a simple, neat conclusion. It's the process that's important, and based on the data collected, you can prepare an interesting display for a science fair that reports your ongoing, unfinished research and the questions that remain to be answered.

THE PROJECT REPORT

If you plan to enter your project in a science fair, or submit it as a class assignment, you should write a detailed report. Using a word-processing program on a computer will allow you to start with a rough outline and add to your report as you get more data. Your report should include an acknowledgment of those who helped you in any way, the problem you investigated and your motivation for pursuing it, a discussion of what you did and why, the results you obtained, experimental errors, conclusions you have drawn based on the data collected and how you arrived at them, and a bibliography consisting of any books, magazines, or Internet resources you used in your research.

Charts, drawings, graphs, and photographs will help make your display more interesting and attractive. Graphs should be plotted with straight lines or smooth curves, but don't connect the points immediately. If you repeat an experiment several times (remember repeatability), the points you plot will cluster, but they won't be at exactly the same place every time because of experimental error. That's why you draw the best line or curve you can through the points.

If you have access to a computer, you can record your results in a spreadsheet program. These programs make it easy to calculate statistics (see Appendix 2). In addition, many spreadsheets include graphing functions to make your data and calculations more visual and easier to understand. Good-looking graphs also stand out in a science fair. And if you make a strong first impression, people walking by will want to find out more. Programs such as *ClarisWorks* or *Microsoft Works* are "all-in-one" programs that contain word-processing, database, spreadsheet, graphing, and drawing functions.

Most expensive "graphing" programs are geared toward business use, but some inexpensive commercial software can help you present your data in graphic form. *Graphical Analysis*, by Vernier Software (2920 S.W. 89th St., Portland, OR 97225,

503-297-5317), is a great program that your school may already have. The school can put it on as many computers as desired for just under $50. The program does "best-fit" graphs and can even come up with a mathematical equation to describe the lines you get. Math teachers and professional scientists who might evaluate your project will be impressed that you included this information. We talk about how to use both spreadsheets and graphs in Appendix 3.

If your results include graphs, the graphs would be a good way to show variation in results due to error. Explain the source of these errors and how they might be reduced. Using some of the statistics outlined in Appendix 2, such as standard deviation, will help you determine which errors are experimental, which are expected due to natural variability, and which differences are great enough to be interesting and worth further research.

Here's a helpful hint: put your bibliographical data in a database program (or module of an "all-in-one" program) as soon as you get it. Set up the database card with a space for the author, title of the book or article and magazine, copyright date, publisher, closest city of publication, the pages you used, and room for quotes or notes. That way things are ready for both footnotes and a bibliography. The Internet is still new to many schools so some teachers may not know how to write a bibliographical entry for Internet information. Here are the forms used most often for MLA-style citations of Internet sources:

<http://www.cas.usf.edu/english/walker/janice.html>

<gopher://info.monash.edu.au: 70/00/handy/cites>

Notice that you give the address (http://, gopher) of the place where you got the information so that anyone viewing your exhibit or reading the accompanying paper can get more information, just as they can with the traditional print sources in your bibliography.

TABLE 1   ACCESSING AN INDEX ON THE WEB

Address	Search engine
http://altavista.digital.com/	AltaVista: Main Page
http://hotbot.com/	HotBot
http://webcrawler.com/	WebCrawler Searching
http://www.excite.com/	Excite Netsearch
http://www.lycos.com/	Lycos, Inc. Home Page
http://www.search.com/	the generic search place from Netscape
http://www.yahoo.com/	Yahoo!

The Internet gives you instant access to even more information at millions of locations around the world. Ask your teacher how to use a "search engine" such as *WebCrawler, Lycos, Yahoo!, HotBot, Excite,* or *AltaVista* to find out about science fairs, contests, free materials, or what other people have done in your area of investigation. You can even contact a "key-pal" or another school class to get information from their locations, such as rainfall amounts or temperatures.

Your science teacher, librarian, or computer teacher can show you how to make your searches more effective by using special language. For example, you might be interested in "active volcanoes," but you'll come up with many strange references if that's your search term. For example, you might come up with travel information for older people who want to "remain active and travel to faraway places like foreign cities, jungles, and volcanoes." With a search engine like AltaVista, you could type "active NEAR volcanoes NOT travel". Then the words "active" and "volcanoes" would have to be near each other and not associated with "travel." There are other tricks involving parentheses and quotation marks that a good "cybrarian" (computer librarian) can teach you to make your search much easier. The Internet Resources section at the back of this book lists dozens of sites that will interest you.

THE SCIENCE FAIR DISPLAY

The display you make for the fair should be attractive, organized, and include some art, if possible. Computer drawing programs (even those in all-in-one programs) can be very useful, allowing detailed work with easy-to-make changes, and even providing you with copyright-free "clip art." If you don't have a color printer at home, your school or a neighborhood copy shop may be able to make color printouts of your pictures. Just be sure to save the final pictures on a floppy disk in a widely used format such as pict, paint, TIF, EPS, or GIF.

With your report, include samples of your data, the plants or animals you used, and your instruments or tools. Examples of your observations and/or results should be part of the display. If practical, judges and visitors might enjoy making a sample run of the experiment you did. Be prepared to talk knowedgably to the judges about your project. Be confident. It's your project, after all, so you probably know more about it than anyone else.

CONTESTS, INTERNSHIPS, AND AWARDS

Each fair, whether local, state, or national, has its own rules and specifications, so read the entry information and application carefully before planning your project. For example, many contests for students below college level forbid the use of any animal with a backbone, eliminating studies of any animal more complicated than an insect. Check the rules *before* you undertake a project for a specific contest. Check with your teacher for information about state and local science fairs. Also look over the list in Appendix 1.

CHAPTER 1

Getting Your Feet Wet

All the projects suggested in this chapter involve water in one form or another. Some include fairly detailed instructions about how to do the experiments; some present questions with few, if any, suggestions as to how you might proceed in answering them. If you have a real flair for scientific investigation and have done a lot of experimenting, you may want to move to these more open-ended projects immediately. On the other hand, if you're new to the art of inquiry, you may prefer to start with projects that provide more guidance. After you get your feet wet, you may feel more confident about designing you own experiments, equipment—and even your own questions.

HOW BIG ARE RAINDROPS?

You can capture, preserve, and measure raindrops by letting them fall into a pan filled with fine flour that is at least 1 inch (2.5 cm) deep. Each drop will form a tiny pellet of dough. In a normal rainstorm, you'll have plenty of samples in just a couple of seconds. After the pellets have dried, you'll be able to measure their diameters with a ruler. (By the way, most scientists make measurements using the metric system: centimeters, meters, grams, kilograms, milliliters, and liters. The metric system is the everyday measurement system in most countries—but not the United States! Because so many countries use the metric system, scientists do too. You can use the metric system in your reports and presentations, and give the English equivalents if you wish.)

If you're beginning to think like a scientist, you might say, "But the raindrops may not be the same size as the pellets of dough." You're right! But you can let drops of known sizes fall into the flour and then measure the pellets formed. You can produce water drops of different sizes with medicine droppers, burettes, and drawn glass tubes.

To measure the volume of a single drop, let several hundred drops fall into a small graduated cylinder or medicine cup. Then find the volume of a single drop by division. How can you find the diameter of a drop if you know its volume? By making a graph of pellet diameter versus drop diameter, you'll be able to find the size of any raindrop. An easy way to record your data is to use a spreadsheet like the one that comes in the "all-in-one" program you probably got with your computer. Programs such as *Microsoft Works*, *ClarisWorks*, *WordPerfect Works*, and *Great Works* all have a spreadsheet module that will record data neatly, allow you to make calculations easily, and even make graphs from the data. This will make your results easier to understand.

In a fine, gentle rain, as long as the drops don't splatter, you can collect droplets on a cookie pan or cardboard sheet covered with waxed paper. Take the pan inside and quickly measure the droplets' diameter with a ruler placed beneath the paper. If the drops are very small, you might want to use a magnifying lens and a ruler to make your measurements. You can see that the drops have become hemispheres on the wax surface. The hemisphere contains the same amount of water—

the same volume—as did the spherical raindrop. How will the diameter of the hemisphere enable you to find the volume of the original raindrop?

As you become skilled at measuring raindrops, you may want to pursue such questions as these: Does the size of the raindrops change as a storm progresses? Are spring raindrops generally larger than those that fall in autumn? Are drops from a light shower larger than those from a steady rain? How many raindrops are in a snowflake? A hailstone?

THE SHAPE OF RAINDROPS

Are raindrops really tear-shaped, the way artists draw them? Design an experiment that will enable you to see raindrops as they fall. A good camera may be useful, but raindrops, like all light bodies falling through the air, reach a uniform, maximum velocity (called the terminal velocity) after a short time; that is, their speed stops increasing because air resistance becomes equal to the force of gravity. If you could suspend them in midair, you could see what they look like as they're falling. A strong, controlled airstream might make this possible.

You can actually see a raindrop with a strobe light or stroboscope. A strobe light flashes a bright light at regular intervals so you see repeated actions as if they were one action frozen in time. A steady stream of water drops could be "frozen" by a strobe light. You can make a stroboscope by cutting slots in a circular disk and mounting it on an axle. Turn the disk at just the right speed with a bright light illuminating the drops from behind, and you'll see the drops. Try photographing the drops in midair.

FALLING DROPS

What does a raindrop look like after it lands? If it falls into water, it produces a "tower." To see what a raindrop looks like if it hits a hard surface, use a medicine dropper to release drops of colored water above a piece of paper resting on a flat surface. Let the drops fall from different heights. Does the pattern made by the splashed drops change as its speed (due to the added height of the fall) increases? Could you use your strobe light or stroboscope to see this better? Could you photograph the action using the techniques from the last section?

What happens to the pattern if the drop is moving horizontally as well as vertically? How does horizontal speed affect the pattern?

Suppose the drop falls on an incline. How will that affect its splash pattern? Design an experiment to find out. Does the steepness of the incline have any effect?

Does the pattern of the splashed drop change if it lands on different surfaces? You can try wood, concrete, aluminum foil, and dirt. By all means try waxed paper: it repels water and makes a splash pattern that is different from those seen on ordinary paper. Can you predict what the pattern will look like?

When a raindrop falls into a glass or pool of water, a "tower" forms.

SAVE A SNOWFLAKE

While you may not have been surprised to learn that raindrops can be captured and measured, you will probably think it's impossible to preserve snowflakes. Yet that's exactly what you can do.

To capture snowflakes, place a number of small glass plates or microscope slides on a flat sheet of wood (a shingle is good) or cardboard. Put the slides in a cold, protected place until they are cold. Try an unheated shed, a freezer, or a covered box. In addition to your slides, put a spray can of clear lacquer in the same location. The aerosol lacquer Krylon, available in paint and art supply stores, works very well.

Snowflakes form many different shapes.

After the glass and lacquer have been chilled below freezing, spray a thin layer of cold lacquer on each piece of glass. Carry the wood or cardboard into the falling snow so that a few flakes collect on each slide. Then put the slides back in the same cold place, and leave them there for several hours until the lacquer is thoroughly dry.

Now, you can bring the dry slides into a warm place and observe the structure of the individual flakes. How many different shapes do you see? What is common to all the flakes? Do different snowstorms produce flakes with distinctly different shapes? Is shape related to temperature? Can you preserve sleet? Can you preserve snowflakes that have already fallen to the ground? Can you preserve the frost patterns that form on windows by spraying the frost with cold lacquer?

ICE KEEPING: THE ART OF INSULATING

Today it's easy to keep food cold; we simply put it in the refrigerator. But before electricity and refrigerators were common in American households, people kept perishable foods in iceboxes. An icebox was an insulated cabinet that held a large chunk of ice and left some space for food. Several times a week an iceman would deliver a large piece of ice to replace the one that had nearly melted.

In winter, large pieces of ice were cut from frozen lakes and ponds. The ice was stored in icehouses, where sawdust was used to cover and insulate it from the heat of summer. These icehouses had no windows to let in sunlight and high roofs so that warm air would rise and escape through vents. The cold air near the ice kept the warmer air from reaching it. On a hot summer day only swimmers and icemen stayed cool. Ice from frozen ponds in Massachusetts was shipped on sailing vessels as far as Calcutta, India. How did they keep it cool for so long?

You can learn a lot about insulation if you design and build your own mini-icehouses. Use identical pieces of ice to test your various ice-cube keepers. If you freeze equal volumes of water in identical medicine cups, small paper cups, plastic pill containers, or other small containers, you can be sure that the chunks of ice are the same size and shape. The time required for the ice to melt is one way to measure the effectiveness of the insulating materials. How can you tell if the ice has melted when it's covered by insulation? If you place a thermometer into the package, the temperature probably won't get above 0°C (32°F) until the ice melts. A laboratory thermometer registers faster than a medicinal thermometer. You can even purchase a thermometer probe that connects to your computer from Vernier Software at 8535 S.W. Beaverton-Hillsdale Highway, Portland, Oregon 97225-2429 or (503) 297-5317. Try their Web page at http://www.vernier.com.

We already mentioned that sawdust is an insulator. You might want to experiment with newspapers, styrofoam, packing materials, or sponges. Or try suspending the ice on a string in a thermos bottle. You can probably design a number of ingenious icehouses of your own. Which one is the best ice-keeper? What would happen if you mixed the sawdust or styrofoam with the water and froze the slurry instead of just putting the insulation around the outside? Does this mixture take longer to melt?

Is the time it takes your ice to melt (stored inside insulated material or frozen with the insulating material) related to the *density* of the insulating material? Try figuring out the density using weight and volume measurements, or look up the values in standard tables. Then try graphing your results as density versus melting time. Is it a straight line graph? A curved line? Is it regular at all? Try using Vernier's *Graphical Analysis* for easy graphing and mathematical analysis of curve shapes.

MELTING ICE

After you become an expert at insulating ice, you might enjoy investigating the opposite: finding ways to make ice melt faster. For example, does the shape of the ice affect its melting rate? To find out, you could freeze the same volume of water in containers of different shapes. In addition to ice cubes, you could make nearly spherical pieces of ice in balloons; ice cones in conical paper cups; cylindrical ice in medicine vials; and wide, short cylinders of ice in the lids from glass jars or plastic containers. Then you can find the time it takes each shape to melt in the same environment. How can you explain your results?

From your investigation of the melting rates of various shapes of ice, can you predict how surface area will affect the rate at which ice melts? Use a spreadsheet, graphing program, and a graphical analysis program to record your predictions and create professional-looking graphics for your science project display and paper.

What effect do you think stirring or crushing will have on the melting rate? Does ice melt faster in air or in water? To answer this question, use identical ice cubes and water that has the same temperature as the air around it. How can you suspend the ice so that it doesn't rest in its own meltwater?

How does the amount of water in which an ice cube is placed affect the melting rate? How about the temperature of the water?

THE HEAT TO MELT ICE

Design an experiment to find out how much heat is required to melt 1 gram (g) of ice.

HEAT FLOW AND SURFACE AREA

If you know how much heat it takes to melt 1 gram of ice, you can calculate the heat needed to melt any mass of ice. Find out the times required to melt pieces of ice with equal mass but different surface areas. Then you can determine how the rate at which heat flows into the ice is affected by surface area. To keep the difference in temperature between the ice and its surroundings constant, use a large volume of water at room temperature. That way, the water temperature will not be significantly changed by the melting ice.

Record your information in a spreadsheet. Use a graphing program to find the clearest way to display your data.

DOES HOT WATER FREEZE FASTER THAN COLD WATER?

You may have heard people say that hot water freezes faster than cold water. After all, hot water is used at hockey rinks to resurface the ice between periods. And some plumbers claim that on very cold days when they are called to repair broken water pipes due to freezing, it's the hot water pipes that freeze first. Does hot water freeze faster than cold water under some conditions? Does the material of the container used for freezing make a difference? Try a metal ice tray versus plastic or wood. As for the plumbers' observation, find out from a physics teacher about the "water hammer" effect and see if that provides an explanation.

HUMIDITY: WATER IN THE AIR

You can't see the water that's dissolved in air, but if you breathe on a cold window, you'll see the moisture in your exhaled air condensing on the glass. Similarly, on a cold winter morning you can see moisture that has condensed and frozen to form frost on a windowpane.

The solubility of moisture in air increases with temperature; so does the solubility of sugar in water. When a certain volume of water holds as much sugar as can be dissolved at a given temperature, we say the solution is saturated. The same is true of the solution formed when water dissolves in air. Table 2 gives the saturation points, in 1 cubic meter (m^3) of air, for several temperatures. More extensive tables can be found in chemistry or physics handbooks or in books on weather.

The mass of water dissolved in 1 cubic meter of air is called the *absolute humidity*. You can determine the absolute humidity by finding the *dewpoint*—the temperature at which moisture begins to condense out of the air.

Put some warm water in a shiny metal can. Add small pieces of ice to the water as you stir it with a thermometer. (Be

TABLE 2 SATURATION POINTS OF SUGAR

Temperature (°C)	Grams of water per cubic meter of air
0 (32°F)	4.8
5 (41°F)	6.8
10 (50°F)	9.3
15 (59°F)	12.7
20 (68°F)	17.1
25 (77°F)	22.8
30 (86°F)	30.0
35 (95°F)	39.2

careful not to breathe on the can.) Record the temperature at which you first see moisture condensing on the shiny surface. That temperature is the dewpoint.

Suppose you first see moisture when the can's temperature is 15°C. That means the air is saturated with moisture at 15°C. At 15°C there are 12.7 g of water in each cubic meter of air. The absolute humidity is therefore 12.7 grams per cubic meter (g/m^3). If the temperature of the air is 25°C, the air could hold as much as 22.8 g/m^3 of water. *Relative humidity* is the ratio of absolute humidity to the maximum amount of water vapor that the air could hold per cubic meter if it were saturated. It is usually expressed as a percent. In this case the relative humidity is $12.7/22.8 = 0.557 = 55.7$ percent.

Now that you know how to find absolute and relative humidity, you can investigate the humidity of the air inside and outside your home or school during different seasons of the year. How does the humidity inside compare with the humidity outside? How do your humidity measurements compare on clear, cloudy, or rainy days? Do humidifiers really increase the water content of the air in a home? Can you measure the effect of a dehumidifier? What is a sling psychrometer? Can you build one? How could you use it to measure relative humidity? Does humidity have anything to do with "wind chill factor"? How do you calculate wind chill factor?

CLIMBING WATER: A WAY TO DEFY GRAVITY

Paper towels can be used to clean up water spills. But why does paper soak up water? If you look at a piece of paper towel or blotting paper under a microscope, you'll see tiny spaces between the wood fibers that make up the paper. Water is attracted to the fibers, and these forces of attraction cause water to rise up the narrow channels.

Put two glass plates together as shown in Figure 1. You'll see that the water level is highest at the end of the glass plates that is farthest from the narrow stick. Why?

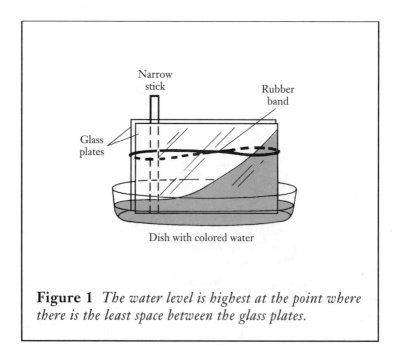

Figure 1 *The water level is highest at the point where there is the least space between the glass plates.*

How high will water "climb" up a paper towel? Cut a piece of paper towel or blotter paper about 1 inch (2.5 cm) wide by 1 foot (30 cm) long. Use a piece of tape to hang the strip from a cabinet, chair, or table so that one end dips into some colored water. (Use a few drops of food coloring.) After several hours you will see that the water has climbed partway up the towel. How high will the water rise?

Repeat the experiment, but this time use several strips of different widths, from 0.125 to 2 inches (0.3 to 5 cm). Does the width of the strip affect the height to which the water rises?

To help you explain these results, repeat the experiment using two identical strips of paper. Cover all but the bottom of one strip with plastic tubing or waxed paper. (You can seal the edges of the waxed paper together with tape to make a tubelike structure.) In which paper strip, covered or uncovered, does water rise higher? Why?

You can also try this experiment with strips of different kinds of paper, cloth, string, blotters, balsawood, or any other materials that you think might work. What do you find? How do you explain your results?

To see if some liquids are more attracted to wood fibers than others, try the experiment using such liquids as alcohol, cooking oil, soapy water, and saltwater, as well as plain water.

IS "BOUNTY" REALLY BETTER?

You've probably seen ads telling you that Bounty-brand towels are better than other paper towels. Is Bounty really a "quicker picker-upper"? Design experiments that will enable you to compare Bounty towels with other brands.

Just what is meant by "better"? Ask a number of people what they think is important in buying a paper towel. Is it the price per square foot? Or how much water each sheet can absorb? Or how much water is absorbed per penny of cost? Or how many grams of water are absorbed per gram of towel? Or how fast a towel absorbs water? Or is it the towel's strength? How do you measure these things?

STREAM TABLES: A MODEL FOR STUDYING WATER FLOW AND EROSION

If your school has a stream table, you can use it to investigate the effects of water flow and speed on various soils, the formation of deltas, the movement of beaches, and various other earth-water interactions that interest you. If you don't have access to a stream table, you can build one as shown in Figure 2.

During the last few years, many communities in the United States have been affected by flooding. Is the level of the rivers and streams in your area dependent on local rainfall? Perhaps the water levels vary with the rainfall in mountains many miles away. Check Internet locations (such as http://www.zebu.uoregon.edu) to find information on local rainfall, river levels, and rainfall in distant places that feed into the rivers. Use a graphing program, such as *Graphical Analysis 2.0*, to graph data from several areas. Computer software allows you to try out various mathematical equations to describe your data and will give you an equation that may allow you to predict what will happen during the next rainfall.

The use of mathematics to predict important events makes it possible to give warnings of possible trouble and so has been extremely valuable to society.

HOW THICK IS A SOAP BUBBLE?

If you've ever blown soap bubbles, you know that they are very thin. But just how thin are they? See if you can figure out several ways to measure the bubbles' thickness. The various methods should all give similar values. As you conduct your experiments, note the colors in the bubbles. What causes the colors? What do the colors tell you about bubble thickness? Check the Internet location http://www.eskimo.com/~billb/amateur/oilfilm.txt for a project dealing with oil-film colors, which have similar wavelengths and thicknesses.

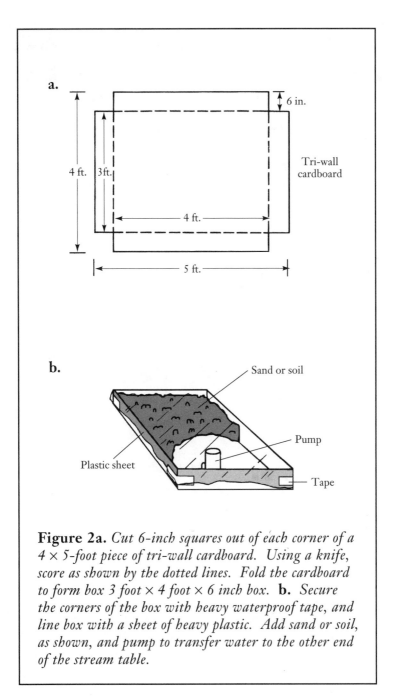

a.

6 in.

4 ft. 3 ft.

Tri-wall
cardboard

4 ft.

5 ft.

b.

Sand or soil

Pump

Plastic sheet

Tape

Figure 2a. *Cut 6-inch squares out of each corner of a 4 × 5-foot piece of tri-wall cardboard. Using a knife, score as shown by the dotted lines. Fold the cardboard to form box 3 foot × 4 foot × 6 inch box.* **b.** *Secure the corners of the box with heavy waterproof tape, and line box with a sheet of heavy plastic. Add sand or soil, as shown, and pump to transfer water to the other end of the stream table.*

WHY DOES A TOY DRINKING BIRD DRINK?

It's fascinating to watch a toy drinking or dipping bird (see Figure 3) "drink" at regular intervals for hours on end. But why does the bird drink? To understand the bird's behavior, try investigating the factors that control the rate at which the bird dips its beak into the water (or other liquids).

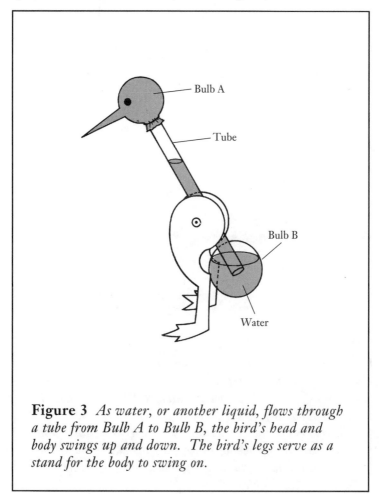

Figure 3 *As water, or another liquid, flows through a tube from Bulb A to Bulb B, the bird's head and body swings up and down. The bird's legs serve as a stand for the body to swing on.*

CHAPTER 2

Astronomy

Don't skip this chapter just because you don't have a telescope. You can do a lot of astronomy without looking through a lens or into a mirror.

Here's one important caution for all astronomical observations: *Never look directly at the sun, even through an optical device! The light is so bright that it can seriously damage your eyes.*

WHICH WAY IS NORTH?

If you live in the continental United States or Canada, you see the sun rise, ascend into the southern sky, and set along the western horizon. You'll never see the sun directly overhead or in the northern sky at midday, but you will see the sun reach its zenith, or maximum altitude, in the southern sky at that time. Because the sun is due south at midday, you can easily establish which direction is true north.

Look at the shadow of a vertical stick late in the morning. Place a marker at the end of the shadow. Using the distance between the stick and this marker as a radius, draw a circle around the stick. Watch the shadow shorten, then mark the direction of the shadow when it is shortest. What is the direction of this shadow? To confirm your measurement, continue to watch the shadow until its end again lies on the circle you drew. Mark this point. Now draw a line connecting the two marks. A line from the stick to the midpoint of the line you just drew should be in the direction of the shadow when it was shortest. Why?

Does midday according to the sun always occur when the clock says it is noon? Why do sun time and clock time differ? Why can't you use a compass needle to find true north in most places?

To further confirm that you've established the direction of true north, see if the line you made points toward a place directly beneath the north star—Polaris. Figure 4 will help you find Polaris. The Big Dipper is easy to find in the northern sky. Its two pointer stars, Dubhe and Merak, are nearly aligned with the north star. With your hand at arm's length, place two fingers on the pointer stars. Polaris will be about five times the distance between the pointer stars in the direction established by Dubhe and Merak. Does the due north direction indicated by the stick's shortest shadow fall under the north star?

Has Polaris always been the north star? Was Polaris the north star when the Egyptians were building pyramids? Will Polaris be the north star 2,000 years from now? Will the constellations change? Would they look different if you were on another planet in our solar system? If you were on a planet orbiting Polaris?

There are a number of astronomy programs for computers, such as *Red Shift*™, *Distant Suns*™, or *Night Sky Interactive*, which will show you the night sky from different times or places in the solar system and galaxy. See if you can detect a pattern in the changes.

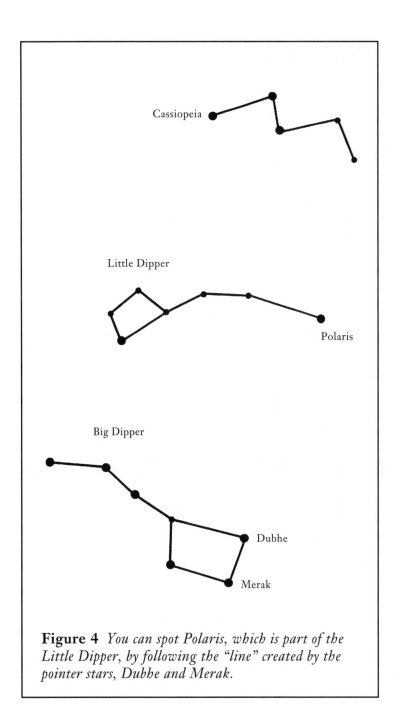

Figure 4 *You can spot Polaris, which is part of the Little Dipper, by following the "line" created by the pointer stars, Dubhe and Merak.*

WATCHING THE NORTHERN SKY

Now that you know how to find true north, you might enjoy watching the stars in the vicinity of Polaris. You can easily identify the constellations shown in Figure 4. Observe them at different times of the night from early evening to dawn. Do their positions in the sky change? Would using a camera on a tripod with the shutter held open help you record changes? How about five or six pictures taken an hour apart? Get help from someone who knows about cameras and try it.

Watch these same constellations from season to season. Are their positions in the sky always the same at the same time each day? Try to explain your observations about these stars in terms of the earth's motion through space.

If you enjoy watching stars, you'll probably want to identify other constellations and observe their paths through the heavens. Not all constellations are visible on every clear night. Some are visible only during certain seasons of the year. Try to explain why some constellations are often hidden from view, while others can be seen every clear night. The astronomy programs mentioned earlier can help you print out a detailed "sky map" of what should be visible from your exact location on a particular night and time. How can you find your latitude and longitude?

MAPPING THE SUN'S PATH

Look up at the sky on a clear day when you're standing in a large open space. You're at the center of what appears to be a huge blue hemisphere. At night, stars glisten like tiny lights set into this now-darkened dome. Astronomers call this dome a celestial hemisphere. The other half of the sky would be seen by someone standing on the other side of the earth. The two hemispheres make up the celestial sphere. Stars and planets appear to follow paths along the celestial hemisphere.

One star's path through the sky is easy to map—our nearest star, the sun. To establish the path of the sun across the sky, you'll need a clear plastic dome and a marker. Put the dome on a piece of white paper with a flat board or sheet of cardboard underneath. Draw a circle around the base of the dome; then remove the dome and mark the exact center of the circle. Replace the dome and tape it to the board. Place it in a level place where it will be in sunlight all day.

The "X" at the center represents you; the dome represents the sky, or celestial hemisphere. To map the sun's path, start as soon after sunrise as possible. Place the tip of the pen on the clear dome so that the shadow of the tip cast by the sun falls on the "X" at the center of the circle. Mark that point on the dome with your pen. As you see in Figure 5, this mark represents the position of the sun in the sky. How do you know the mark is in line with the center "X" and the sun?

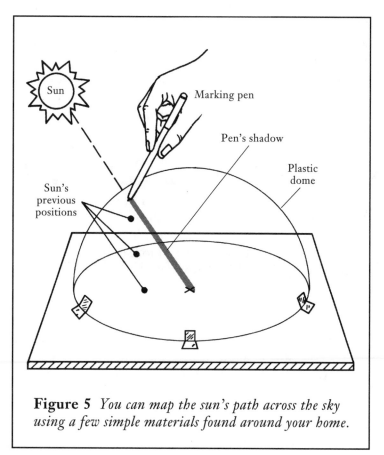

Figure 5 *You can map the sun's path across the sky using a few simple materials found around your home.*

Continue to make marks like this every hour or half hour throughout the day. By evening you will have a pattern that maps the sun's path along the celestial hemisphere.

If you mark north on this dome, you can use it to map the sun's path across the sky at various times during the year. Or you can use a different dome each time. Try to map the sun's path at the beginning of each season. What dates mark the start of spring, summer, autumn, and winter? How does the sun's path along the sky change from season to season?

Using your solar maps and observing shadows at sunrise and sunset, try to determine the direction of sunrise and sunset at various times of the year. Does the sun always rise in the east and set in the west? When is sunrise due east? Try to explain why the sun's position in the sky changes during the year. You might make a model of the earth and sun using a ball and a lightbulb in a large, dark room.

Go to the library, or use an Internet search engine to investigate the astronomy of the Stonehenge monument in England. Do any other very old monuments show that ancient people knew about astronomy?

MOON MAPPING AND WATCHING

The moon's path across the sky is more difficult to map because the moon casts less distinct shadows and is often seen in the daytime sky. With an astrolabe, like the one shown in Figure 6, you can determine the moon's altitude at various times of the night or day. Also, you can observe its rising and setting positions along the horizon. (Telescopic observations of the moon are interesting too.)

As with the sun, map the moon's path across the sky over a year's time. You'll see that the moon's shape undergoes periodic and predictable changes. Collect as much data as you can every day. Why does the moon's path change so much faster than the sun's?

How do you explain the changes in the moon's appearance and celestial path? A model of the sun, moon, and earth may help you explain your data. If a full moon rises around 6:00

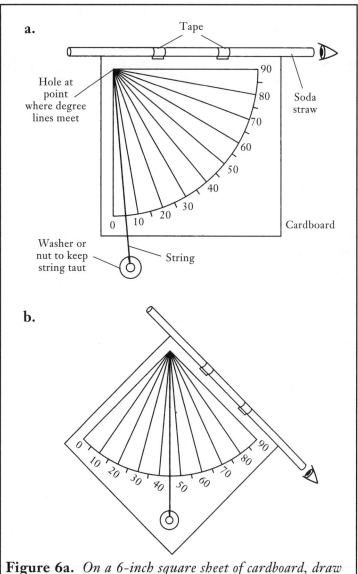

a.

Tape

Hole at point where degree lines meet

Soda straw

90
80
70
60
50
40
30
20
10
0

Cardboard

Washer or nut to keep string taut

String

b.

0
10
20
30
40
50
60
70
80
90

Figure 6a. *On a 6-inch square sheet of cardboard, draw angles at 5° intervals with a protactor. At the point where the degree lines meet, punch a tiny hole with a needle and thread a thin string through the hole.* **b.** *In this case, the moon is at an altitude of approximately 45°.*

P.M., will a quarter moon rise at the same time? What time *must* a new moon rise? Your model should help you decide.

THE SIZE OF THE SUN AND MOON

Use a pin to make a tiny hole in the center of a piece of black construction paper. If you let sunlight pass through the hole onto a white screen held beneath the black paper, you'll see a pinhole image of the sun. To prove that this really is an image, move the screen closer to and farther from the pinhole. What happens to the size of the image?

Cut a tiny square and triangle in the same black paper. Do these holes also produce round images? Why does a tiny pinhole produce an image of the sun? Can you make pinhole images of other light sources, such as a candle flame or a lightbulb?

Once you've explained why pinhole images form, see if you can use a pinhole image to measure the diameter of the sun, knowing that the sun is, on the average, 93 million miles (150 million km) from earth. With a full moon, you might be able to use the same method to measure the moon's diameter. However, since you can look directly at the moon, matching the moon's diameter with the diameter of an object held a known distance from your eye will allow you to use similar triangles to find the diameter of the moon, which is about 240,000 miles (386,000 km) from the earth, although the distance varies from 225,000 to 252,000 miles (362,000 to 405,000 km).

Something else you might want to investigate is the *apparent* size of the moon. The full moon always looks huge when it rises in the evening near the horizon. Later on that same night, does it look nearly as large? Devise a way to see if the size really changes. If it doesn't, why does it appear to change?

A GLOBAL VIEW OF EARTH

Put a large globe outdoors in a place where it will be in sunlight all day. A large empty can will provide good support for the globe, as shown in Figure 7. Arrange the globe so that it

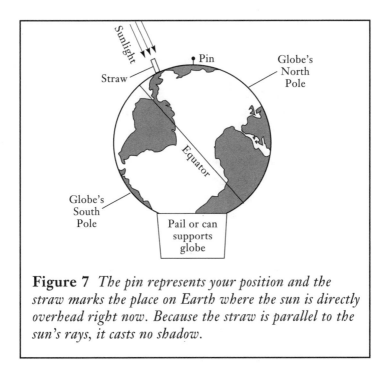

Figure 7 *The pin represents your position and the straw marks the place on Earth where the sun is directly overhead right now. Because the straw is parallel to the sun's rays, it casts no shadow.*

represents the way you see the earth; that is, with your location at the very top of the globe. Then turn the globe so that its north pole points at Polaris. As long as your hometown is at the very top, why will the globe's north pole automatically be directed toward Polaris when its poles are along a north-south axis?

Stick a pin in a bit of clay at the top of the globe to represent you. The pin's shadow on the globe should be parallel to your shadow on the ground.

The globe provides a view of what Earth would look like from far out in space. From this view, where on earth is the sun rising right now? Where is the sun setting? Where is it dark? Are there places, near one of the poles, where the sun will not rise at all today? Are there places, near the other pole, where the sun will never set today? What time is it now in Chicago? San Francisco? Honolulu? Oslo? Peking? Tokyo? Athens? Check your conclusions with a computer program such as *Small Blue Planet*. If your computer's clock and date keeper have been set correctly, you should be able to see the sun line just the way it is on your model.

A perpendicular object won't cast a shadow if the sun is directly overhead. Use a short piece of soda straw with a pin through it to locate a place on Earth where the sun is directly overhead right now. Try to predict where the sun will be directly overhead one hour from now. Test your prediction an hour later. Were you right?

Watch the globe throughout the day. As the day progresses, what happens to the western parts of the globe that are near the edge of darkness?

Using a ball to represent the moon, find out where it is relative to the earth and sun today. Where is the moon relative to you, the earth, and the sun when it is full? When it's a new moon? Repeat your observations at different times of the year. What changes do you notice?

What else can you learn from this global view of earth? How did the Greek astronomer Eratosthenes find the earth's diameter? Use the Internet or your library to find out.

A SIMPLE TELESCOPE

Build a simple telescope with a pair of lenses and some mail tubing. Find the focal length of each lens. Arrange the lenses relative to their focal lengths to get the greatest magnification. Determine the magnification of your telescope. Can a program such as *Graphical Analysis* help you determine a formula for finding the magnification of any telescope once you know the length of the tube and the focal length of the lenses? Try it and then compare your results to those shown in a high-school physics book.

COUNTING STARS

When you look into the sky on a clear, cold night, it seems as though there are millions of stars in the sky. But how many can you really see?

To estimate the number of visible stars, you can count the stars in sample areas of the sky and then multiply to find the number expected for the entire area of the celestial hemisphere.

Cut a square 4 inches (10 cm) on a side from the center of a large cardboard sheet. Hold the sheet exactly 12 inches (30 cm) in front of your eyes. Keeping your head very still, count all the distinct stars you can see within the square hole. The area through which you are viewing the stars is $\frac{1}{57}$ the total area of the sky; therefore, if you multiply the number of stars you counted by 57, you should have the total number of stars visible in the celestial hemisphere.

Why is the area of the sky you are viewing $\frac{1}{57}$ the total area of the hemisphere? Would it be more accurate to make several

On a clear, cold night, the sky is filled with untold numbers of stars.

counts of the stars in the square while viewing different parts of the sky, and take an average before multiplying by 57?

Count the number of visible stars. Would you find more or fewer visible stars if the sky were hazy? If you looked through a telescope? If you included the Milky Way? Use an astronomy program for your computer, like *Distant Suns*™ or *Red Shift*™, to show all the stars of fourth magnitude, fifth magnitude, and sixth magnitude. Sixth magnitude is usually the limit for naked-eye observing. Then use the programs to show you the dimmer stars and check the results by using binoculars or a small telescope. What's the dimmest magnitude you can see with your eyes alone? How about with binoculars?

THE ART OF ESTIMATING

When you counted the stars in the sky, you used a technique called estimation. Estimating is useful in science because often we want to know the number of things that are too numerous to count individually.

See if you can devise estimating techniques to find the number of: blades of grass in a lawn, beans in a large jar, leaves on a tree, hot dogs eaten in the United States in one year, or molecules of water in a glass. How about the amount of paint needed to cover your house, the weight of grass seed needed to plant a lawn, and the number of shingles needed to cover your roof.

One technique scientists now use in estimation involves mathematics that a computer can perform. Try filling several small jars with beans and making actual counts of the number of beans. Then find the volume of the jars using a measuring cup or, better yet, a graduated cylinder. Now graph these measurements using a graphing program and try to extrapolate to larger jars. Or, use a program like *Graphical Analysis* to come up with a mathematical formula for your estimate. Then try a larger jar and see if your formula works.

CHAPTER 3

Let the Light Shine In

Light is essential to our existence, not only because objects are visible solely from the light they *reflect*, but also because, without light, plants could not manufacture food. Many people live without being able to see, but no one can live without food.

A STRANGE REFLECTION: SQUARE TO CIRCLE

Use a square or rectangular mirror to reflect a beam of sunlight. Hold a screen close to the mirror. The reflected beam forms a square patch of light on the screen. But what happens to the size and shape of the light patch as you move the screen away from the mirror? Look at the light patch on the side of a building 100 or 200 feet (30 or 60 m) away. What shape is the reflected patch? Why?

CURVED MIRRORS

Not all mirrors are flat. A shaving or makeup mirror has a concave shape like a saucer. The side mirrors on some cars and the mirrors in many stores are convex. They have a slight domelike shape.

A concave mirror, as you might expect, will bring parallel rays of light together. In fact, if you hold a concave mirror some distance from a window, you can form an image of what you see through the window on a white sheet of cardboard held in front of, and slightly to one side of, the mirror. Move the cardboard back and forth until the image is clear. Unlike images formed in a plane mirror, these images are actually on the screen. They are called *real images*, and that's why you can "capture" them on a screen. You can't do that with the images seen in a plane mirror; that's why those images are called *virtual images*. But why is the real image upside down? Is it also reversed right for left?

A *focal length* is defined as that distance from the concave mirror at which parallel rays of light are brought together. Coming from a point on a distant object, the rays of light that reach a concave mirror must be nearly parallel; therefore, the point where the light rays come together (forming an image) is nearly one focal length from the mirror. The point where these rays meet is called the *principal focus* of the mirror. Why are the light rays from a distant object that strike the mirror almost parallel?

Find the focal length of your concave mirror. Then place a small lighted bulb such as a flashlight bulb at a position greater than one focal length from the reflecting surface of the mirror (Figure 8). Where is the image of the bulb found? What happens to the image position if you move the bulb two focal lengths from the mirror? three focal lengths? four? Still farther?

Now place the bulb between the principal focus and mirror. Try positioning the bulb one-half of a focal length from the mirror. Where is the image now?

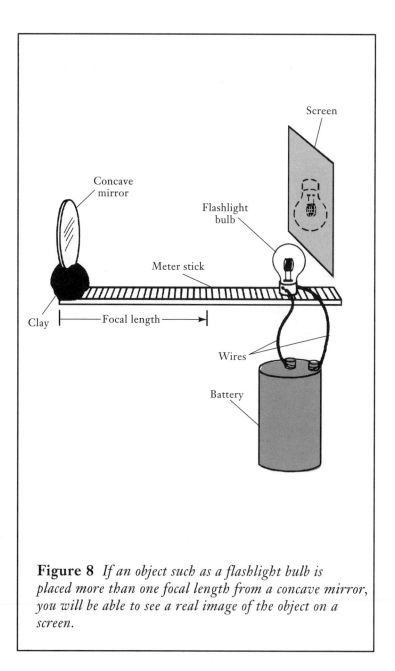

Figure 8 *If an object such as a flashlight bulb is placed more than one focal length from a concave mirror, you will be able to see a real image of the object on a screen.*

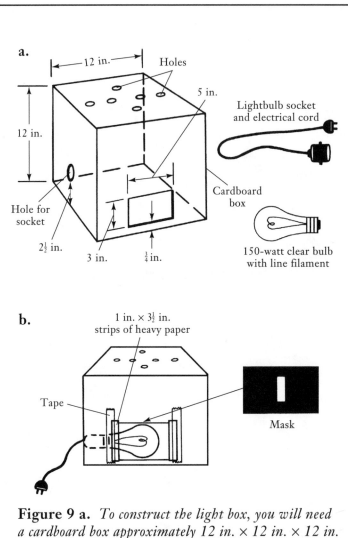

a. 12 in. ← Holes

12 in.

5 in.

Lightbulb socket and electrical cord

Hole for socket

$2\frac{1}{2}$ in.

3 in. $\frac{3}{4}$ in.

Cardboard box

150-watt clear bulb with line filament

b. 1 in. × $3\frac{1}{2}$ in. strips of heavy paper

Tape

Mask

Figure 9 a. *To construct the light box, you will need a cardboard box approximately 12 in. × 12 in. × 12 in. with holes in the top (so heat from the bulb can escape) and a lightbulb socket attached to an electrical cord.* **b.** *Insert the bulb with the socket sticking through a hole in the side of the box. A mask of black construction paper will be taped over a 3 in. × 5 in. hole in the side of the box.*

Now investigate the image positions of an object seen in a concave mirror. How do the position and size of these images change as the object is moved?

To understand the images formed by plane, concave, and convex mirrors, you might want to design and build a ray-maker or light box like the one shown in Figure 9. You can use the light box to make light rays and see what happens to them when they strike plane mirrors and two-dimensional concave and convex reflecting surfaces.

Try to form some mathematical relationships among object distance, image distance, focal length, object size, and image size for concave and, perhaps, convex mirrors.

BENDING LIGHT

Use a small piece of clay to support a plane mirror that has been placed on a piece of white paper attached to a sheet of cardboard. Mark the edge of the mirror so that it can be replaced if it is accidentally moved. Use two pins (A and B) to establish a line (ray) of light to the mirror. To mark the reflected ray, place two more pins (C and D) in line with the images of the first two pins as shown in Figure 10a. Use a ruler and pencil to mark the rays of light. You now have an incident ray (going to the mirror) and a reflected ray (coming from the mirror). How does the angle between the incident ray and the surface of the mirror compare with the angle between the reflected ray and the mirror's surface? Would the results be the same for all incident and reflected rays?

Now that you know how to make incident and reflected rays, repeat the experiment, but this time let the light reflect from the mirror *after* passing through water and a clear plastic or glass container (Figure 10b). Where do these rays meet? Could the reflection have taken place in front of the mirror? How do you explain these results? Design an experiment to test your hypothesis. You might use the light box in Figure 9 in your experiment.

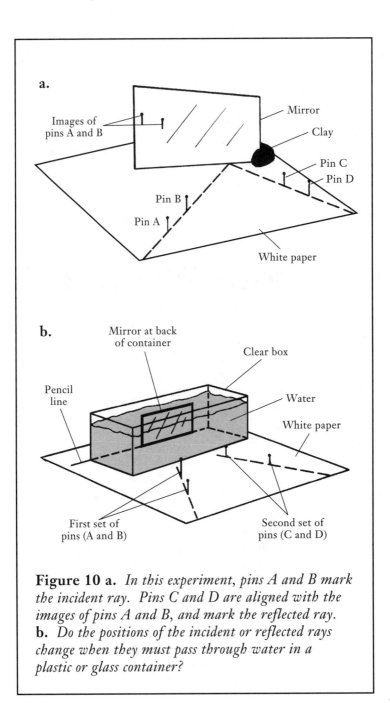

a. Images of pins A and B

Mirror

Clay

Pin C

Pin D

Pin B

Pin A

White paper

b. Mirror at back of container

Clear box

Pencil line

Water

White paper

First set of pins (A and B)

Second set of pins (C and D)

Figure 10 a. *In this experiment, pins A and B mark the incident ray. Pins C and D are aligned with the images of pins A and B, and mark the reflected ray.* **b.** *Do the positions of the incident or reflected rays change when they must pass through water in a plastic or glass container?*

SIMPLE MICROSCOPES

Use a pair of convex lenses to build a simple microscope. Should one lens have a shorter focal length than the other? See if you can figure out how these lenses work to create a magnified image. You might take a look at a commercial microscope to see how it is built.

Try making a simple microscope using a drop of water as a lens. Try other liquids. Which liquid works best? An early developer of the microscope, Anton van Leeuwenhoek, used drops of glass for his lenses. Can you find out more about him and make a microscope using the same simple tools he had?

CYLINDRICAL LENSES AND TRIANGULAR PRISMS

Jars and vials of water can serve as two-dimensional models of lenses. With a light box to create rays and a cylinder of water to serve as a lens, you can investigate the way convex lenses form images. You can even change the amount the light is bent by adding sugar to the water.

Here's a fun experiment to try on your friends. Fill two clear plastic pill bottles with hot water. Add a drop of blue food coloring to one and a drop of red food coloring to the other. On a piece of paper write the words "OXIDE" and "SPACE." Place the blue bottle horizontally over the word "OXIDE." Slowly raise it until you get a clear image. Use the red bottle to view the word "SPACE." Is either word inverted? If so, why? Is it because of the color of the water?

If you let a ray of light enter a glass or plastic prism, you can expect it to *refract* the light, but you may be surprised to find that it bends some colors more than others. Which colored light is refracted the most? Which color is refracted least? Is there a similar effect with lenses? Look carefully. Does the difference in the way colors are refracted have any effect on the focal length of different colors of light? How might this affect our perception of depth? Do artists use this effect to create depth in paintings?

For a project, you might develop a test of depth perception to use on others. Collect your data and put the results in a spreadsheet. Figure the standard deviation (see Appendix 2). Collect data about your subjects to see if there is any correlation between depth perception ability and age, color of eyes, height, distance between the eyes, or another factor. A graphing program like *Graphical Analysis* may allow you to show a correlation you can include in your project.

MIRAGES, REFLECTION, AND REFRACTION

Many mirages, such as the apparent presence of water on a hot paved road, inverted ships on the sea, or pools of water in the desert, are the result of reflection and/or refraction. Try to observe these phenomena. Can you explain these mirages using what you know about reflection and refraction of light?

MIXING COLORED LIGHT

Using mirrors, the light box shown in Figure 9, and colored filters, you can transmit beams of red, blue, and green light. (Good light filters can be obtained from Rosco Laboratories, Inc., 36 Bush Avenue, Port Chester, NY 10573. Order medium red #823, medium blue #863, and medium green #874.) Camera stores sell filters too, but they can be expensive. Look for a mail order house like Freestyle Photo Sales, 5124 Sunset Blvd., Los Angeles, CA 90027-5708, http://www.free-style-salesco.com for cheaper prices. Use a mirror to reflect red light onto a green light beam viewed on white paper. You'll find that the mixture is yellow. Red and blue light produce magenta, and green and blue give cyan. Try to make white light from these colored beams.

Place a pencil near the light box so it casts a shadow along one of the light beams. What could you do to give part of the shadow a yellow color? A cyan color? A magenta color? Try to give the shadow colored stripes. Where have you seen colored shadows before?

When you think you understand the mixing of colored light, cover the stage of each of three overhead projectors with a piece of cardboard. At the center of each cardboard sheet, cut a circular opening 3 to 4 inches (8 to 10 cm) in diameter. Cover each opening with a sheet of different colored plastic—red, blue, and green—so you can shine circles of the primary colors on a white screen. Predict the color of your hand's shadow held in any beam and illuminated by each or any combination of the colored light beams.

Suppose you hold your hand in a red beam of light casting a shadow on the screen illuminated by white light. You may be surprised to find that the shadow is cyan, not black. What color is the shadow cast by a green light when illuminated by white light? How about the shadow cast by blue light when illuminated by white light?

Is this an illusion? To find out, photograph the shadows with color film. What do you find? Explain this effect.

INVESTIGATING SHADOWS

Not all shadows are colored, but they are usually interesting.

Watch shadows change during the course of a day. Watch as the shadows of poles, buildings, and other objects change their midday length during the course of a year. Watch the direction of morning and evening shadows change from season to season. Note where shadows are fuzzy and where they are sharp. See how they change when cast by different lights. Look for multiple shadows, for funny shadows, for overlapping shadows, and shadows shaped differently than the objects that cast them. There's no end to investigating shadows or the questions your observations will raise.

In the late afternoon, shadows grow long and often have interesting and beautiful shapes.

COLORED OBJECTS IN COLORED LIGHT

A blue object is blue because it reflects only blue light; it absorbs other colors such as green and red. Why then is an object yellow? magenta? cyan? black? white? To check your hypothesis, see if you can predict what color small pieces of colored construction paper will appear to have when viewed in different colored lights.

Now answer the question, "Why is a green leaf green?" Then try growing some pea plants indoors using only light of specific colors. Try green, blue, red, violet, and yellow lights. Put the results on a spreadsheet, figure the standard deviation (see Appendix 2), and graph the results. Are there "statistically significant" differences? Can you explain the results?

PINHOLE IMAGES

Cover an opening in a light box with a piece of black construction paper. Use a pin to punch a tiny hole in the paper. Now hold a white screen near the hole. You should see an image of the lightbulb's filament. What happens to the size of the image as you move the screen away from the box? Explain this image. Is it inverted? Is it reversed right for left? How can you find out?

What happens if you punch a second hole in the paper? What effect does the size of the pinhole have on the image?

Using a large box and the pinhole method, you can make a good-sized image of the sun that you can view in semidarkness. See if you can make the image large enough to see sunspots.

Take a small piece of aluminum foil and make a needle hole in it. Hold this in front of your eye. Using a bright object or small print, measure how close your eye can focus with and without your "pinhole magnifier." Now try making a hole with a larger needle and measure the distances. Does the size of the hole make a difference? Can you find a correlation between the focus distance of your eye and the size of the needle used? Look in a sewing store for a package of needles with different sizes. If the sizes aren't marked, talk to a science or shop teacher and find out how to use a micrometer to measure the sizes.

MAKING RAINBOWS

A diffraction grating is a piece of glass or plastic with many very fine parallel scratches. Some of the white light passing through the narrow slits between the scratches is separated into a spectrum revealing all the colors that make up white light. (Diffraction grating material can be obtained from Edmund Scientific, 101 E. Gloucester Pike, Barrington, NJ 08007.)

With the large box that you used to make a pinhole image of the sun, mount a diffraction grating over a small opening cut in one end of the box near the top. At the other end, on each side of the square patch of light that comes straight through the grating, you'll see a rainbowlike spectrum, made by the sun's white light passing through the grating. Can you see a similar "rainbow" using the grating and a light box? Try to explain why light passing though a grating creates a spectrum.

Using prisms, mirrors, bubble makers, containers of water, garden hoses, and sunlight, see how many different ways you can make rainbows. Then try to explain how a natural rainbow is made.

CAN LIGHT BE BENT WITH MAGNETS?

You've seen that light can be bent from its normal straight-line path using water, glass, or a diffraction grating. Do you think a strong magnetic field will deflect a light beam? To find out, let a narrow beam of light, such as a laser beam, pass between the poles of a strong magnet. Mark the position of the light on a distant screen, then remove and replace the magnet. Is light deflected by the magnet?

Laser light can be harmful to human eyes, so when you use a laser, be sure to follow these safety rules. Never look into the laser beam. Even reflected laser light can be dangerous. Don't look at laser light reflected from a shiny surface. Don't let the laser light pass through windows where it might accidentally strike someone's eyes. Lock the door or post a warning outside the room where you are experimenting so that anyone entering isn't at risk of having laser light enter his or her eyes.

Lightning lasts for only a fraction of a minute, but it is possible to capture its image forever on film.

PHOTOGRAPHING LIGHTNING

To capture the beautiful zigzag pattern of lightning flashes, set up a camera on a tripod near a window through which you can see lightning at night. Turn off all inside lights and aim the camera at the active clouds. After several minutes, you'll develop a feel for when the next flash will occur. Set the camera at f/16 and focus on infinity. Anticipate the stroke by a few seconds and make 20- to 30-second exposures.

CHAPTER 4

Chemistry

Chemistry is concerned with the structure of matter and the way different kinds of matter combine or decompose. It's an exciting part of science, but it can also be very dangerous. Before trying any of the projects in this chapter, read the following paragraph and the safety information in the Introduction.

Always do chemistry experiments under the supervision of a knowledgeable adult (like your science teacher) and in an environment conducive to safety. Always wear safety goggles while performing chemistry experiments! Even if experiments don't involve chemicals and seem like they can be done without supervision, check with your science teacher or another adult before you start. You can never be too careful when doing chemistry experiments.

HOW MUCH OXYGEN IS THERE IN AIR?

Some books tell us that the following experiment can be done to find out what fraction of the air is oxygen. Try it for yourself. Use a small lump of clay to hold a birthday candle upright in a shallow dish of water. When the candle has burned for several minutes, cover it with a tall, narrow glass jar, like the jar green olives come in. Measure how high the water rises after the candle goes out. How does the height of the water level compare with the total height of the jar? The ratio of these two heights will give you the percentage of the air that is oxygen.

Repeat this experiment a few times. Do you get the same results each time? If you don't, do several trials, put the results in a spreadsheet, and figure out your best answer, with the standard deviation to show your confidence level. Put a little soap in the water and notice the bubbles that form when you place the jar over the candle. What do you think causes the bubbles?

Here's another way to measure the percentage of oxygen in air. Place a small, loosely rolled ball of steel wool in a solution of one part vinegar to two parts water. Let it soak overnight to remove the protective coating on the steel. Shake off the excess liquid and push the steel ball to the bottom of a tall, narrow jar. Invert the jar in a dish of shallow, colored water so the mouth of the jar is below the water level. Leave the jar in this position for 24 hours. What happens? Leave it for another day to see if there are further changes. Look at the steel wool carefully. What has happened?

According to this experiment, what fraction of the air is oxygen? Repeat the experiment several times. Are the results consistent? If not, take the results of several trials, put them in a spreadsheet, and figure out your best answer, with the standard deviation to show your confidence level. What causes water to rise in the jar? Which method really measures the percentage of oxygen in air? What evidence do you have to support your decision? Carry out any additional experiments to support your position.

WEIGHING GASES

Weigh an empty plastic bag and a twist tie. Fill the bag with air, tie it shut with the band, and reweigh it. How much does the air appear to weigh? Why? If you have trouble explaining your result, ask yourself this question: How much do you weigh when you float in water? Look up "Archimedes" in the library or on the Internet.

Invent a method that will allow you to weigh air and other gases.

Once you've found a way to weigh gases, see if you can predict the results of this experiment. Place some water in the bottom of a long balloon. Use a twist tie to seal the water off from the rest of the balloon. Pour some Bromo-seltzer or pieces of Alka-seltzer into the upper part of the balloon above the water. Tie off the top of the balloon and hang it from one end of a sensitive balance. Remove the band that separates the seltzer from the water so that the seltzer falls into the water. What happens? Does the apparent mass of the balloon and its contents increase, decrease, or remain the same?

IDENTIFYING METALS

Collect a number of metal samples about 10 cubic centimeters (cm^3) or larger in size. You'll also need a reference table that gives the properties of various metals. You can find this information in a handbook of chemistry and physics or in a physics or chemistry textbook. You can also find a lot of information about constants used in physics and chemistry at this Internet address: http://physics.nist.gov/Phys/RefData/codata86/codata86.html. Information about individual elements is available at: http://mwanal.lanl.gov/julie/imagemap/periodic.html.

Find the density and specific heat of each metal. With that information can you identify all of the metals? If not, what additional information would be helpful?

SEPARATING A MIXTURE

Add the following substances to a jar: 50 milliliters (ml) of water, 25 ml of methyl alcohol, some sand, some charcoal, a teaspoon of salt, and a couple of drops of black ink or food coloring. Stir the mixture.

Design a method for separating the components of this mixture. Explain the method to your science teacher or another knowledgeable adult and ask permission to begin your experimental work.

TITRATING HOUSEHOLD LIQUIDS

The vinegar and ammonia that you buy in a store are both about 1 molar (1 M) in concentration; that is, they contain 1 mole of the solute (acetic acid or ammonia) per liter of solution. Using standardized solutions of sodium hydroxide and hydrochloric acid, as well as appropriate indicators and burettes, determine the actual concentration of ammonia in household ammonia. Does the concentration of acid in the vinegar agree with the percentage value on the label? Try several different brands of vinegar and several different bottles of the same brand, bought a month or two apart so that they come from different batches. How do the concentrations compare?

Purchase a variety of commercial antacids. What volume of 1 M hydrochloric acid (HCl)—the concentration in your stomach—can be neutralized by 1 g of each antacid? Is the dissolving rate of various antacids in plain water the same as it is inside your stomach?

ACID RAIN

Much has been written about acid rain. But did you know that rain is normally acidic? Carbon dioxide in the air dissolves in raindrops, giving them a pH between 5 and 6. (A pH value less than 7 is acidic.)

Using sensitive pH strips, titration, or a pH meter, test samples of rainwater. Does its pH change as a storm progresses? Does the pH of rain vary from season to season? Is geography related to acid rain; that is, does the pH of rain vary with location? Is snow acidic?

For a further test, compare the acidity of fresh rainwater with the acidity of rainwater after it soaked into typical soil for your region or the soil around lakes. Using a network of "key-pals"—science students from other parts of the country—compare your results, put them in a spreadsheet, and graph them. Color them by their representative pHs. This is easiest to do with a computer program that allows you to "fill" areas with different colors. Pick a color scheme to represent increasing acidity. You can use the colors found on the box of pH paper.

For your local area, the pH of rainwater won't change much, but how about the acidity or alkalinity of soil? Is it different at the bottom of a hill or at the top? How about in a farmer's field, around your house, in the ground under trees, or near a river?

Computer probes, such as those from Vernier Software can be used to measure pH quickly and accurately. Portable, hand-held electronic pH meters are now available at a low price.

ACID-BASE INDICATORS

To test a solution's acidity or alkalinity, you may have used litmus paper, pH paper, or indicators such as bromthymol blue or phenolphthalein. Early chemists used natural indicators that came from fruits and vegetables.

To see an example of this, pour some unsweetened grape juice into a glass. Dilute about 1:9 with water to reduce the color intensity. Add a drop or two of household ammonia to some of the diluted grape juice. What color is grape juice in a base? Now add vinegar until the color of the liquid changes. What color is grape juice in an acid? *Do not drink this or any other solution you make.*

You can prepare extracts for testing from the skins of radishes, peaches, tomatoes, rhubarb, red apples, and turnips, or from red cabbage, red onions, cherries, beets, or blueberries. Chop each material in a blender. Remove the chopped skin, fruit, or vegetable and place it in a beaker. Cover the extract with distilled water and warm (don't boil) the mixture for an hour. Pour off the liquid into another beaker. Dilute with water if necessary.

Add 1 M HCl to the extract you have prepared until the pH falls to 2 as indicated by a pH meter, pH test papers, or a computer hooked up with pH test probes. Slowly add a dilute solution of NaOH drop by drop, recording color and pH as you go. Would any material or combination of materials that you tried make a universal indicator?

SPEEDY ALKA-SELTZER

Watch what happens when you drop an Alka-seltzer tablet into a glass of water. The bubbles you see are formed by gas. You can measure the rate of the reaction by collecting the gas in a graduated cylinder and calculating how fast it's produced.

What gas is produced when Alka-seltzer reacts with water? Which ingredients in these tablets are responsible for producing the gas?

When you drop an Alka-seltzer tablet in a glass of water, it dissolves and releases a gas.

Design and carry out experiments to see how each of the following factors affects the rate of the reaction: temperature, concentration of reactants, concentration of products, pressure, and surface area of reactants. What do you find? Put your results in a spreadsheet and graph them. Better still, graph them with *Graphical Analysis* and try different equations to see if you can find a mathematical relationship that describes your findings.

THE THICKNESS OF ALUMINUM FOIL

Cut a piece of aluminum about 10 cm on a side from a roll of heavy-duty aluminum foil. Cut another piece from a roll of thinner aluminum foil. Weigh both samples to the nearest 0.01 g. Determine the area of both sheets. The density of aluminum is 2.7 g/cm^3. What is the volume of each sheet? Using its volume and area, determine the thickness of each sheet.

HOW BIG IS A MOLECULE?

You've probably seen the rainbow-colored film that forms when a thin layer of motor oil floats on a puddle of water. Some substances that are insoluble in, and less dense than, water will spread out into a very thin layer on water. One such substance is oleic acid. If you could determine the thickness of an oleic acid layer on water, you would have an estimate of the maximum size of a molecule of this oily substance. If the layer spreads out until it is one molecule thick, your estimate could be quite close to the actual size of an oleic acid molecule.

To make this estimate, pour water into a large, flat tray (such as the kind found in cafeterias), until the water is about 1 centimeter deep. When the water is still, sprinkle a fine, powdery layer of chalk dust on its surface. You can do this by rubbing a piece of chalk over sandpaper or by rubbing your finger along a used blackboard eraser. Next, bend a fine piece of wire into a narrow V-shape. Wind the upper ends of the wire together and use a clothespin to hold the wire. Dip the V into some alcohol to clean it. When it's dry, dip only the very tip of the V into some oleic acid. You want only a tiny drop of the liquid to cling to the wire.

Make a rough estimate of the drop's volume by asking someone to hold the clothespin while you use a magnifying glass and ruler to estimate the diameter of the drop. By assuming that the drop is either a cube or a sphere, you will be able to estimate its volume.

Dip the tip of the wire into the center of the water. You will see the oleic acid spread, pushing the fine powder outward and leaving a circle that defines the size of the oleic acid layer. Dip the wire tip into the water several times to be sure all the oleic acid has been transferred. Measure the average diameter of the oleic acid layer on the water.

Calculate the oleic acid's volume and its area on the water. You can then determine the thickness of the layer and, therefore, the maximum height of an oleic acid molecule. What do you find? If you assume the molecules are cube-shaped, how many molecules were in the tiny drop? If these molecules were arranged end to end, how many times would they wrap around the earth?

Find the density of oleic acid. What was the mass of the tiny droplet? Based on your data, what is the mass of an oleic acid molecule? The actual mass of an oleic acid molecule is 4.7×10^{-22} g. If you're using a scientific calculator or a computer spreadsheet to do your calculations, the number may appear as 4.7 E-22. (If you don't understand this terminology—called scientific notation—look in a good science or math textbook.) How close were you? What was the major source of error in this experiment?

To obtain a more accurate value for the volume of oleic acid that was placed on the water, you can dissolve 5 ml of oleic acid in 95 ml of alcohol. Then take 5 ml of this solution and mix it with 45 ml of alcohol. After calibrating a medicine dropper so you know how many drops of oleic acid are in 1 ml, use the dropper to place 1 drop of the dilute oleic acid on a water surface as before. Predict the diameter of the layer when you add a second drop.

What is the maximum thickness of a molecule this time?

Design an experiment to show that it's oleic acid and not alcohol that accounts for the displacement of the fine powder on the water in this experiment.

OXIDATION AND THE CORROSION OF IRON

Oxidation is defined as the loss of electrons by an atom or ion. Of course, we can't see electrons being transferred from one atom to another, but we do see the effects of oxidation when large numbers of atoms are oxidized. For example, we recognize that iron has been oxidized when we see the rust that results from this process. If iron is oxidized from the metallic state to ferrous ions, we can explain that reaction by the equation below:

$$Fe \rightarrow Fe^{++} + 2e^-$$

If one substance loses electrons, another must gain them. A substance that gains electrons is said to be reduced. For example, when iron rusts or corrodes, the electrons its atoms lose may be gained by either hydrogen ions or oxygen and water molecules as shown by these equations:

$$2H^+ + 2e^- \rightarrow H_2 \quad \text{or} \quad O_2 + 2H_2O + 4e^- \rightarrow 4OH^-$$

The presence of ferrous ions can be detected with the compound potassium ferricyanide $[K_3Fe(CN)_6]$, which reacts with ferrous ions to form the deep-blue precipitate ferrous ferricyanide, $Fe_3[Fe(CN)_6]_2$. If hydroxide ions form, they can be detected by the indicator phenolphthalein, which turns pink in a basic solution. You can use these chemical tests to investigate the corrosion of iron. ***Don't forget to wear your safety goggles!***

Heat approximately 200 ml of water in a 400-ml beaker. When the water is boiling, add 2 g of agar-agar powder while stirring constantly. Once the agar has dissolved, remove from heat and add the following indicators: about 10 drops of 0.10 M potassium ferricyanide and 10 drops of phenolphthalein, which is made by dissolving 1 g of powdered phenolphthalein in 50 ml of water and 50 ml of ethyl (denatured) alcohol.

While the agar is cooling, place two shiny iron nails that you have cleaned with steel wool in each of two petri dishes. In the first dish, bend the nail with a pair of pliers. In the second dish, wrap the nail tightly with a piece of heavy copper wire, leaving plenty of space between the wire turns; wrap the other nail with a strip of zinc about 3 mm wide. You can cut the strip from a thin sheet of zinc.

Once the agar is lukewarm but not jelled, pour it into the two dishes so that the nails are completely covered. Allow the agar to harden as you watch for any indication of oxidation and reduction around the nails. Examine the nails periodically and record your observations. What is the effect of working the metal? (Note what has happened at the tips, heads, and center of the bent nail.) How does zinc affect the oxidation of iron? How about copper? How do you explain your results?

Try to predict other metals that would prevent the oxidation of an iron nail. Test your predictions experimentally.

CHAPTER 5

Physics

Galileo and Newton changed the study of our natural world from philosophical discussion to experimental inquiry. They are the fathers of modern science and the first to find the basic patterns in the chaos of motion. It was Galileo who revealed to the world that all falling bodies, if air resistance is negligible, accelerate at the same rate as they fall near the earth's surface. And it was Galileo who made it clear that the vertical and horizontal motion of a projectile, be it cannonball or baseball, are independent of one another.

But it was Newton who demonstrated that a falling body is merely one example of the effect of gravitational forces that cause all masses to attract one another. And it was Newton who revealed that the acceleration acquired by an object is proportional to the force acting on the object, and inversely proportional to the object's mass.

A balance is one of the most valuable tools in science. Figure 11 shows how to build a simple balance.

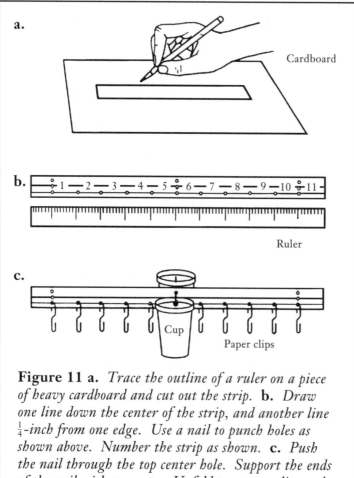

Figure 11 a. *Trace the outline of a ruler on a piece of heavy cardboard and cut out the strip.* **b.** *Draw one line down the center of the strip, and another line $\frac{1}{4}$-inch from one edge. Use a nail to punch holes as shown above. Number the strip as shown.* **c.** *Push the nail through the top center hole. Support the ends of the nail with two cups. Unfold ten paper clips and put them in the holes along the bottom of the cardboard strip. If the strip isn't level, trim a little cardboard off the heavy end.*

When you've made the balance, get a dozen or more identical steel washers. By hanging various combinations of washers on the cardboard strip, see if you can find a rule to help you balance the strip. For example, if someone hangs two washers 3 inches from the center of the strip on the right side and three washers 2 inches from the same point, can you use your formula to predict where to hang three washers so the "balance beam" will be level?

To discover the rule, conduct a lot of trials, put the numbers in a computer spreadsheet, and graph the results. If the rule isn't easy to see right away, export your spreadsheet data to a graphing computer program and try different equations to see if you can get a straight line graph.

When you think you've mastered this problem, invite a friend to play a game of "balance." Hang some washers on one side of the balance. Then hand your friend a fixed number of washers and challenge him or her to balance the cardboard beam in one move. Now let your friend challenge you.

Do you think the position of the nail (the fulcrum) at the center of the cardboard strip has any effect on the balance? To find out, set up the balance as shown in Figure 12. Use the

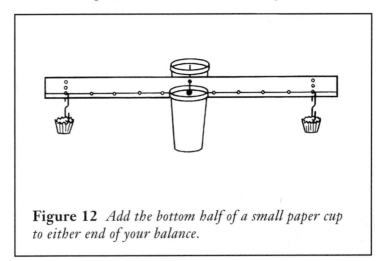

Figure 12 *Add the bottom half of a small paper cup to either end of your balance.*

bottom half of small paper cups as "pans." If the beam isn't quite level, add a little clay to the pan on the lighter side. With the nail through the top center hole, how many drops of water can you add to one balance pan before it touches the table? Repeat the experiment with the nail through the middle hole and again with the nail through the lower hole. In which position is the balance most sensitive (most responsive to added weight)?

Does the position from which the pans at the ends of the beam are suspended have any effect on the sensitivity of the balance? How about the distance of the pans from the center of the beam? How about the mass of the object being weighed?

Try to explain why the sensitivity of the balance is affected by the factors you've investigated. Then design and build a sturdier balance so that you can weigh objects to at least the nearest hundredth of a gram. Can you build a balance that will weigh light objects to the nearest thousandth of a gram?

AN INCLINED PLANE

An inclined plane is one type of simple machine. But how does an inclined plane make *work* easier?

To find out, hang a heavy toy truck or laboratory cart from a spring balance. How much does the cart weigh? Place the cart on a board tipped at an angle above a level floor or table, as shown in Figure 13 on the next page. Measure the force, along a direction parallel to the board, required to support the cart when the board is tipped at various angles. How is the force required to support the cart related to the angle between the board and the table or floor? Put your data in a spreadsheet and graph the results to make them easier to understand.

How does the work required to lift the cart to a certain height compare with the work required to pull the truck along an incline to the same height? Do inclined planes make it possible or us to do less work, or do they make our work easier?

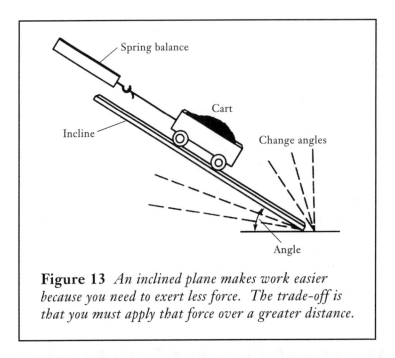

Figure 13 *An inclined plane makes work easier because you need to exert less force. The trade-off is that you must apply that force over a greater distance.*

THE SLIPPERY SUBJECT OF FRICTION

The only way you can walk is to push against the earth's surface. When you push against the ground, the earth pushes back against your foot. It's that force on your foot that accelerates you forward. If you've ever tried to walk along an icy sidewalk or a polished floor, you know it's a difficult task. You can't push as hard as you can when you walk on a concrete sidewalk because there's very little friction between your feet and the ice or a polished floor. *Friction* is always present when one surface rubs against another. Sometimes the force of friction is large; sometimes it's very small.

With the setup shown in Figure 14, you can measure the frictional force when various surfaces rub together. Use washers or weights to measure the force needed to make a block slide across a level surface at a constant speed. The force opposing the force you apply to the block is friction. What would happen to the speed of the block if you pulled on it and there was no friction?

Tape different kinds of material to the block and record the force needed to move it for each run. You could also try placing waxed paper, aluminum foil, newspaper, cardboard, sandpaper, or strips of felt or other cloth on the tabletop. Try putting rubber bands around the block, thumbtacks into the

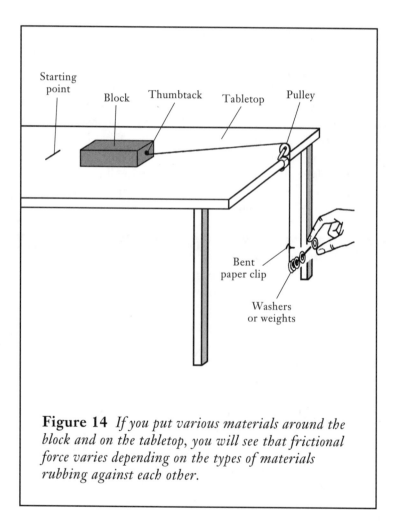

Figure 14 *If you put various materials around the block and on the tabletop, you will see that frictional force varies depending on the types of materials rubbing against each other.*

block, or round pencils under the block. Which combination of surfaces produces the most friction? Which combination gives the least friction? What if you made the surface a piece of street asphalt and tried pieces of tires with different tread designs? A local tire store can probably give you pieces of different tires. What about making the surface a layer of ice in a shallow pan and trying a regular-tire tread, snow-tire tread, or tires with steel studs, aluminum studs, and chains?

How does the weight of the block affect friction? If you place a second block on the one you are pulling, does the force required to move the block at constant speed double? Does the area of contact between the block and the board affect the friction between the surfaces? Is starting friction (the force needed to get the block moving) greater than kinetic friction (the force needed to keep the block moving at constant speed)?

How could you determine the frictional force by lifting the board and measuring the angle between the board and the floor when the block slides at a constant speed? In all these tests, you can keep the data you collect in a computer spreadsheet and graph your results to help you see what is happening.

ROLLING WHEELS, SLIDING WHEELS

Watch a slowly moving automobile closely when the driver applies the brakes. Do the front or rear brakes grab first?

Find a toy car with wheels that turn freely. Watch it roll down a smooth incline such as a wide board as you raise the board. Next, use two strong rubber bands to secure both the front and rear wheels so that they cannot turn. (The brakes are locked.) Place the car on the incline again. Does it move more or less easily than before? Why?

Remove the rubber band from the front wheels so that only the rear wheels are locked. Again, place the car on the incline and watch it descend. What happens? Finally, let the car go down the incline with the front wheels locked and the rear ones free to turn. What happens this time? How do you explain these differences? What does this experiment have to do with your observation on automobile brakes?

LAUNCHING AND MAPPING PROJECTILES

Drop a ball. It falls because the force of gravity pulls it toward the center of the earth. If you throw a ball, it travels in a curved path because it moves horizontally as it falls. Galileo said that these horizontal and vertical motions are independent. This means that if you throw one ball horizontally and drop another one from the same height, both balls will strike the ground at the same time.

To analyze projectile motion, build a ramp that will launch marbles horizontally. Figure 15 on the next page shows you how to build this launching pad. Let a marble roll down the ramp. Just as it leaves the edge of the ruler, drop another marble from exactly the same height. Do both marbles reach the floor at the same time? If they do, you'll hear one "thud" instead of two. Repeat the experiment several times. What do you find? Does it matter if the marbles have different weights?

Does the height from which you release the marble on the ramp affect the distance it travels horizontally?

Let a marble roll down the ramp from different heights. To see how far it travels horizontally before reaching the floor, tape white paper to the floor around the vicinity where the marble lands. Cover the white paper with carbon paper so that the marble will leave a mark when it strikes the paper. Does the height of the marble's release on the ramp affect the distance it travels horizontally? If you double the vertical height of release, does the horizontal distance double? You can get computer controlled "timing gates" that use beams of light to tell how fast your projectile is traveling as it leaves the launch point. They can automatically send the results to a spreadsheet for further calculations.

Plot a graph of the horizontal distance traveled by the marble versus the height from which it was released. Can you find a relationship between these two variables? Of course, using a computer graphing program will make it easier to draw the graph. Using a program like *Graphical Analysis* will make it easier to discover a mathematical rule to explain your data.

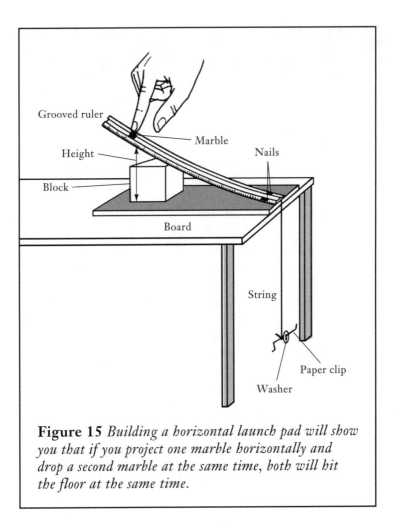

Grooved ruler

Marble

Height

Nails

Block

Board

String

Paper clip

Washer

Figure 15 *Building a horizontal launch pad will show you that if you project one marble horizontally and drop a second marble at the same time, both will hit the floor at the same time.*

If the launcher is higher above the floor, will the horizontal distance the marble travels before it lands change? Does tilting the ramp up or down affect the horizontal distance the marble travels?

By placing the launching pad near a wall, you can map the path of the projectile. Tape a large sheet of white paper to the wall. Have a friend release the marble from the top of the ramp. Draw a vertical line with a pencil 3 to 4 inches (8 to 10 cm) from the end of the ramp. Watch the marble as it passes the line. Make a short horizontal line at the point where you think the marble crosses the vertical line. Check it several times by watching the marble as it moves across the lines. Repeat this process at several places along the marble's path.

When you have plenty of points, connect them with a colored marker or crayon. Watch the marble as it moves down the end of the ramp to the floor. It should closely follow the path you've marked.

What is the shape of the path? What does the shape tell you about the horizontal and vertical speeds of the marble as it moves? How could you measure these speeds at different times into the marble's flight? Will a larger marble or a steel ball follow the same path?

Using a strobe light, a tripod, and a camera that can have its shutter held open, you can take a picture of the ball's path. Make sure the strobe light flashes at least five times while the ball travels from the end of the ramp to the floor. A white marble in front of a black background in a dark room should show the path quite well.

A BASEBALL PROJECTILE

Galileo showed us that a projectile—a ball, bullet, or other object thrown or shot into the air—will maintain a constant horizontal speed as it *accelerates* vertically due to gravity. To see this for yourself, drop a water balloon or a sealed bag of sand as you ride a bicycle over a target marked on a sidewalk. If you drop the bag when it's directly above the target, does it fall on the target? Where should you drop it if it is to hit the target?

You might also drop a tennis ball as you walk. Do you have to stop to catch the ball? Or does the ball maintain the horizontal speed it had because it was in your hand? Where do you find the ball if you do stop walking after releasing it?

You can use what Galileo taught us to measure the average force you exert when you throw a baseball. When you throw a baseball, you do work on it and it acquires kinetic energy. Its kinetic energy (KE) is equal to the product of the average force (F) that you exert and the distance (d) through which that force acts. How can you measure the distance (d)?

The kinetic energy of the ball is given by:

$$KE = F \times d = \tfrac{1}{2} mv^2 = \tfrac{1}{2} m(v_x^2 + v_y^2)$$

In this equation, v_x is the horizontal velocity of the ball, v_y is the vertical velocity of the ball at the moment it is thrown, and m is the mass of the ball.

You can determine the horizontal velocity of the ball by measuring the distance it travels horizontally and the time it took to travel that distance. Use a stopwatch to measure the flight time of the ball. Since the acceleration due to gravity (g) is 9.8 meters per second per second (m/s²) for all bodies, if we ignore air resistance, we can find the vertical velocity from the equation:

$$2V_v = gt,$$

where t is the total time the ball is in the air. What is the average force that you exerted on the ball?

Estimate the time it took to throw the ball. To check your estimate, you can calculate the time it took to throw the ball once you know the momentum (mv) of the ball at the moment it was released (t) and the average force (F) that you exerted:

$$mv = F \times t$$

How close was your estimated time to the time you calculated?

Throw a ball straight up into the air. If you know the time it takes for the ball to return to your hand, you can calculate the speed of the ball at the moment you released it.

Have some of your friends hit a pitched ball. For each fly ball or line drive determine the horizontal distance the ball travels and its time of flight. From that data, calculate the velocity of the ball and the angle that the ball's path makes with the horizontal as it leaves the bat. You can use a computer timing gate or a radar gun to check how accurate your estimates are.

What path angle gives the ball its greatest distance for any given velocity? What error is introduced by measuring the distance to the point where the ball strikes the ground?

EGG DROPS

There's no replacement cost involved in throwing or dropping baseballs; these spheres don't normally break or shatter. But what about eggs?

Design a container into which you can place an egg, drop it from a second or third story onto a concrete sidewalk, and end up with an egg that's not cracked or broken. When you've perfected your container, you might want to enter or sponsor an egg-dropping contest.

BOUNCING BALLS

Have you heard that the bounciness of old tennis balls can be restored by heating them? Design an experiment to test this idea. You might also see if temperature has an effect on the bounciness of other balls—baseballs, lacrosse balls, golf balls, and, of course, Super Balls.

Do different kinds of balls differ significantly in their bounciness? Does the surface on which they bounce have an effect? Why won't a ball bounce to a height greater than the height from which it was dropped? Test your hypothesis.

PENDULUMS AND SPRINGS

Galileo realized that the to-and-fro motion of a pendulum could be used to keep time. But what makes a pendulum run fast or slow? And how can such a clock be adjusted to keep proper time?

Build a pendulum as shown in Figure 16 on the next page. You can change the mass of the *bob* by adding more washers to the paper clip. You can change the length of the pendulum by changing the length of the string. The amplitude of the swing can be changed by pulling the bob farther to one side before releasing it.

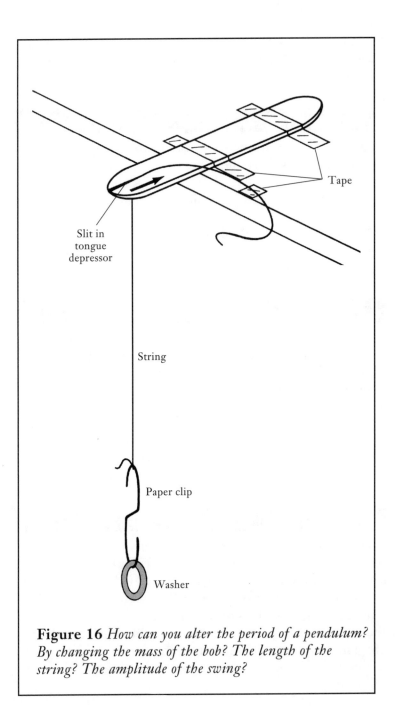

Tape

Slit in
tongue
depressor

String

Paper clip

Washer

Figure 16 *How can you alter the period of a pendulum?
By changing the mass of the bob? The length of the
string? The amplitude of the swing?*

To measure the *period* of a pendulum—the time it takes to make one complete swing, over and back—count the number of swings in 30 seconds or 1 minute and then divide the time by the number of swings. You can also measure the time and speed of the pendulum with a computer interface for a timing gate. Put your data in a spreadsheet and graph it.

Design experiments to find out how the period of a pendulum is related to the mass of the bob, to the length of the pendulum, and to the amplitude of the swing. What do you find? Again, a computer program like *Graphical Analysis* will help you see relationships and write mathematical equations.

Hang a spring, such as a screen-door spring, from a support. Then hang a mass, such as a 1-kg weight, from the bottom of the spring. If you release the mass, you will see that it bounces up and down with a constant period. Is the period of this oscillating spring, like the period of a pendulum, independent of the mass that is hung on it? How is the period of the spring related to the mass it supports? Do different springs have the same period if they support the same mass?

AN UNDECIDED SPRING

Hang a mass on a spring and watch the mass oscillate up and down. Keep adjusting the mass until you find a *critical mass*—one that causes the spring to change from an up-and-down to a back-and-forth (pendulumlike) motion and then back again.

After you've watched this "undecided" spring for a while, see if you can develop an explanation for its undecided mode of motion. How can you test your hypothesis?

BUILDING A BETTER KITE OR PAPER AIRPLANE

Many people like to build and fly kites and/or paper airplanes. You might want to try your hand at building the world's best kite or paper airplane. (Or maybe you'll settle for the best in your state or city.) Keep your eye out for a kite-building or paper-airplane building contest as you explore the art and science of kite and paper-airplane design and construction.

IS YOUR BICYCLE EFFICIENT?

The *efficiency* of a machine is defined as the ratio of the energy or work put out by the machine to the work or energy put into it.

Is your bicycle an efficient machine? Design a method for testing its efficiency. If your bike has gears, does the efficiency depend upon which gear the bike is in? Does it depend upon the weight of the rider? On tire pressure?

CHAPTER 6

Heat: A Form of Energy

If you live in a region where the winters are cold, you'll hear people, perhaps your own parents, talking about heating costs. Homes and apartments in the United States and Canada are usually heated by burning oil, coal, wood, or natural gas, or with the heat supplied by electricity or the sun. Of course, electricity often comes from power plants that burn coal, oil, or natural gas. In all these cases, energy in one form, be it the chemical energy stored in fossil fuels, the radiant energy in sunlight, or electrical energy, is changed into thermal energy, or heat.

The cost of heating your home depends on many factors: the size of the house, how cold it is outside, how warm it is inside, how warm you want it to be inside, how long the house must be heated to reach the desired temperature, and how well the house is insulated.

People have used heat throughout history, but it was only 200 years ago that scientists such as Joseph Black and Benjamin Thompson began to investigate heat to understand what it was and how it behaved.

Caution: Many of the projects in this chapter MUST be conducted under the supervision of your science teacher or another knowledgeable adult. Before beginning, ask your teacher whether it's safe to do the project alone. Always wear safety goggles and handle hot objects and liquids carefully. Work in a clean, neat space to minimize fire hazard.

THE HEAT TO MELT ICE

Joseph Black, a Scottish chemist, lived in the eighteenth century when scientists were struggling to understand the nature of heat. Black observed that ice and snow melt very slowly with no change in temperature. Yet, when snow melted in his bare hands, he could feel huge amounts of heat being released. Black wanted to find how much heat was required to melt a fixed amount of ice. You can perform an experiment similar to his to answer his question.

Black compared the heat needed to melt ice with the heat required to warm an equal weight of water 8°F (4.5°C). He poured equal amounts of water into two containers. He froze the water in one container; he cooled the water in the second container to the freezing point (32°F or 0°C). He then placed both containers, one with ice at 32°F (0°C), the other with water at the same temperature, in a large room where the temperature remained at 47°F (8°C) throughout the experiment. After half an hour, the temperature of the water had risen to 40°F (4.5°C). Ten hours passed before the same mass of ice melted and reached the same temperature. Try such an experiment yourself. Do you get similar results?

Black reasoned that the same amount of heat would enter both the water and ice in the same amount of time. They were in the same room and had about the same amount of area exposed to the warmer air. In view of the relative times to bring both samples to 40°F (4.5°C), Black argued that it required about twenty times as much heat to melt ice as it did to raise the temperature of water 8°F (4.5°C). Do you agree with Black's reasoning?

It takes 1 calorie to raise the temperature of 1 g of water 1°C. One BTU (British thermal unit) is the heat required to raise the temperature of 1 pound of water 1°F. How much heat, in calories, is required to melt 1 g of ice? How many BTUs of heat are required to melt 1 pound of ice?

Design an experiment of your own to find the heat needed to melt a fixed weight of ice.

Why did Black measure the time it took for the water to reach 40°F (4.5°C) rather than 47°F (8°C), which was the temperature of the room? To help answer this question, you might try plotting a graph of the temperature of ice water as it warms up to room temperature versus time. How is the flow of heat from one substance to another related to the temperature difference between them?

Design an experiment to measure the heat required to boil away a gram or a pound of water. How do you think Joseph Black would have done this?

You can improve the accuracy of this experiment, and *any* experiment involving temperature changes, by using an electronic thermometer connected to a computer. Temperature probes allow you to read temperatures several times a second with an accuracy of one hundredth of a degree. These readings can automatically be put into a spreadsheet and a graphing program to give you a continuous graph of the temperature changes. Try Vernier Software's *Data Logger* program connected to some temperature probes. Their Universal Lab Interface package may already be part of your science teacher's supplies. With that interface, you can measure acceleration, temperature, movement, force, pressure, pH, heart rate, respiration, and many other variables.

CALORIC MASS

Joseph Black didn't attempt to explain what heat is. He was content to learn, through experimentation, how it behaves. Other scientists theorized that heat is an invisible fluid, which they called *caloric*. They thought that caloric flowed from warm bodies, which were warm because they possessed abundant caloric, to cooler bodies that had less caloric.

Benjamin Thompson (Count Rumford) thought about the caloric theory and Black's experiments that revealed the large amounts of heat required to melt ice, and suggested that if heat really is an invisible fluid, then ice should weigh less than the water from which it is formed. Explain Thompson's argument. Then design an experiment to test his reasoning based on the caloric theory. What do you find?

If you'd like to know how Thompson investigated this idea, read *Count Rumford, Physicist Extraordinary* by Sanborn C. Brown (Anchor Books, 1962).

HOW HOT IS A FLAME?

If you try to measure the temperature of a flame by putting a thermometer into it, you will succeed only in breaking the thermometer. You need a less direct method for finding the temperature of something as hot as a flame.

One approach is to heat a piece of metal in a flame until it has the same temperature as the flame. Then add the metal to some water and record the temperature change. (Temperature changes are often written as ΔT. The symbol Δ is the Greek letter delta. It's often used in mathematics and science to mean "change in." The temperature difference between two temperature readings T_2 and T_1 can be expressed as $T_2 - T_1$ or as ΔT.) If you know the mass of the water and its temperature change, you can determine the amount of heat transferred from the metal to the water. Since the heat gained by the water was lost by the metal, these two heats can be set equal to each other. If you know the kind of metal you're using, you can find its specific heat, $heat_{sp}$ from a table and solve this equation:

Heat loss by metal = Heat gained by water

$$Mass_{metal} \times heat_{sp} \times \Delta T_{metal} = mass_{H_2O} \times \Delta T_{H_2O}$$

$$Mass_{metal} \times heat_{sp} \times (T_{flame} - T_{final}) = mass_{H_2O} \times (T_{final} - T_{initial})$$

The only thing you don't know in this equation is the temperature of the flame, which you can easily calculate.

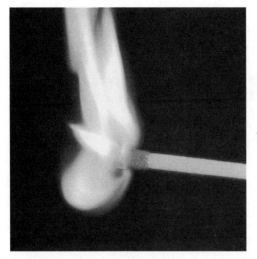

When you strike a match, a chemical reaction occurs between the substance on the match head and oxygen in the air. The products of that reaction include light and heat.

To do the experiment you'll need a flame, a small piece of metal that will fit in the flame (a small steel washer is fine), an insulated cup, cold water, something to hold the washer in the flame, and a thermometer that will measure to the nearest 0.1°C or a computer temperature probe. Wear safety goggles and be careful with flames and hot objects.

Determine the mass of the piece of metal. Then hold the metal in the flame for several minutes. You can use an unfolded paperclip, held by a clothespin outside the flame, to support the metal. Once the metal is hot, have a friend place a small volume of cold water in an insulated cup and measure the water's temperature. Remove the thermometer (unless you're using the temperature probe) and quickly (so as not to lose heat to the air) drop the metal into the water. Stir the water and record the final temperature.

Repeat the experiment several times. How did you decide how long to heat the metal? How much water should you use? What is the temperature of the flame?

Use this technique to determine the temperatures of a variety of flames. You might test the flames of alcohol burners, bunsen burners, candles, gas stoves, and matches. Which flame is hottest? Why do you think the flames have different temperatures?

You can check your results by using a *thermocouple probe* hooked up to a computer. (It is available from Vernier Software for about $35.00.)

HEAT LOSS AND SURFACE AREA

Heating costs depend in part on the size of your house. But heat can escape only from the surface of a house, so you might guess that heat losses or gains are related to the surface area of your home.

To test this idea, make two pieces of ice that have the same volume but different surface areas. Because the ice pieces are made with the same mass of water, it will take the same amount of heat to melt each of them. It takes 80 calories, 334 joules, or 0.31 BTU to melt 1 g of ice. How much heat is required to melt each piece of the ice you made?

Once the ice pieces are thoroughly frozen, fill a bucket or large container with water. Use a lot of water to melt the ice so that the water temperature doesn't change significantly; after all, the temperature difference between the ice and the water could affect the melting rate. After measuring the dimensions of the ice pieces so you can calculate their surface areas, drop the ice into the water. Stir the water constantly so that the surfaces of both pieces of ice will be in contact with the water and not their own meltwater. After 10 seconds remove both pieces of ice and quickly dry and weigh them.

How much ice melted from each piece? How much heat flowed into one of the ice pieces per second? How much heat flowed into the other piece of ice per second? What was the surface area of each piece of ice? Compare the two ratios:

Heat flow into ice piece #1 in one second
Heat flow into ice piece #2 in one second

Area of ice piece #1
Area of ice piece #2

What do you find? What does that tell you about the rate of heat flow and surface area? Why didn't you simply wait until all the ice had melted and then calculate the heat flow per second? How will the heating costs of a house with a large surface area compare to one with a small surface area if all other factors are the same?

HEAT LOSS AND TEMPERATURE DIFFERENCE

From experience, you know that the rate at which heat flows from your body depends on the temperature of the air or water around you. If you step outside on a cold day, you'll soon begin to shiver unless you're wearing warm clothing. Shivering makes your muscles work, producing more heat in your body. On a hot day, you sweat and heat is absorbed from your body to vaporize the perspiration.

To see how the temperature difference between two substances affects heat flow, pour 100 ml of hot water into each of two cups. The temperature of the water in the two cups should be the same. Leave one cup in a warm room; put the other one in a cold place such as a refrigerator or a protected place outdoors, if it's cold outside. Record the temperature of the water in each container at 1-minute intervals. At some point in your investigation, record the air temperature around each container.

A computer with a pair of temperature probes would make taking these measurements easy. The thin wires of the probes can fit easily through a closed refrigerator door. Vernier Software even makes a set of four probes with 100-foot wires that could be used to take temperatures outside while the computer is inside. You can set the computer data recorder to take readings every minute or even every second. You can use other temperature probes to record the air temperatures while you're measuring the water temperatures.

To see how the cooling rates compare, plot a graph with temperature on the vertical axis versus time on the horizontal axis. Plot both sets of data on the same set of axes. Temperature probe software will do this automatically or you can record your manual measurements in a spreadsheet for computer graphing. How does the temperature difference between the water and air affect the rate of heat loss?

Using either of the curves you plotted, you can determine the slope of the graph at a series of points. Using these slopes, the temperatures, and the mass of the water, plot a graph of the rate of heat loss versus the difference in temperature between the water and its surroundings. A program like *Data Logger* will do this automatically using the probe data, or you can use *Graphical Analysis* with the data you entered by hand to get a curve and an equation for the data. What does this graph tell you?

Design an experiment, using identical ice cubes and large volumes of warm and cold water, to see how the ratio of the melting rates in the warm and cold water compares with the ratio of the temperature difference between the ice and the water in which it melts. Since the melting rate is proportional to the rate at which heat flows into the ice, you are really comparing the rate of heat flow with the temperature difference between the ice and the heat source. What do your results reveal?

INSULATION AND R VALUES

Heat loss or heat flow, as you have seen from these experiments, is proportional to surface area and the temperature difference between warm and cold substances. Heat loss is also related to time. If the temperature difference and surface area between two substances remain constant, twice as much heat will flow in twice the time. One other factor is important in measuring heat loss: the conductivity of the material that lies between the warm and cold substances. Thus, heat loss, ΔH, can be calculated from the equation:

$$\Delta H = U \times a \times t \times (T_{in} - T_{out})$$

where U is conductivity, a is area, t is time, and T is temperature.

Engineers in the United States measure conductivity in units of

$$\frac{0.5 \text{ BTU}}{h \times ft^2 \times °F}$$

Suppose a warm air space surrounded by 10 square feet of $\frac{3}{4}$-inch fiberboard loses 50 BTUs of heat per hour when the temperature of the warm air is 10°F higher than the cooler surrounding air. The conductivity, U, of the fiberboard would be

$$U = \frac{50 \text{ BTU}}{1h \times 10 \text{ ft}^2 \times 10°F} = \frac{0.5 \text{ BTU}}{h \times \text{ft}^2 \times °F}$$

Home owners want insulating materials that do *not* conduct heat well; consequently, insulating materials are rated according to their resistance to conducting heat. A material's ability to resist heat flow is measured in terms of its R value, which is just the inverse of conductivity:

$$R = 1/U$$

The conductivity of the fiberboard above is 0.5 BTU/h × ft² × °F. Its R value would be

$$R = 1/U = 1/0.5 = 2 \text{ ft}^2\text{-h-}°F/\text{BTU}$$

The conductivity is inverted so the numbers that consumers use is greater than 1. A material with a large R value is a good insulator.

Here's a way to measure the R value of cardboard. Put a 100-watt lightbulb in a large, sealed cardboard box resting on a couple of small blocks so that the entire surface of the box is exposed to the cooler air around it. Place the bulb of a thermometer or a temperature probe through the box about halfway up one side so that you can measure the average temperature inside the box. Another thermometer or probe can be used to measure the air temperature outside the box.

When the temperature inside the box becomes constant, we can assume that the heat loss from the box equals the rate at which heat is being generated by the bulb inside. We know the heat generated is 100 joules per second because it is a 100-watt bulb and, if the box is well sealed to prevent light from escaping, any energy that appears as light will be transformed to thermal energy when absorbed by the materials within. Using this information, the area of the box, the temperatures inside and outside the box, and the time (1 second), determine the R value of the cardboard.

Does it make any difference if the cardboard is painted white or black on the inside? If it's painted black or white on the outside? If you test this, make sure you do one trial for black and one for white to determine if paint alone might affect the R value.

Now that you know the R value of a certain thickness of cardboard, you can determine the R values of other materials by comparing the rate at which they lose heat with that of an equal area of cardboard. What is the R value of the styrofoam in coffee cups? What about the R values of other insulating materials such as fiberglass, rock wool, cellulose, vermiculite, newspapers, glass, and wood? How is the R value related to the thickness of a material?

How do your R values compare with those found in books on home energy or with information available from a lumber store or on the Internet?

What are degree days? Using what you know about heat loss and degree days, calculate the heat losses from your home or school over a 1-year period. Translate that into the money needed to buy fuel to supply the heat. How could heat loss and, therefore, heating costs, be reduced in your home or school?

HEATING WITH COLORED SOLAR ENERGY

You know that the energy in sunlight can be converted into heat. You probably also know that the white light of sunlight can be broken up into all the colors of the rainbow. But does the color of the light that falls on a solar collector have any effect on the amount of heat produced? Design an experiment to answer that question.

A MODEL SOLAR HOME OR WATER HEATER

Some homes are heated partially, or even entirely, by energy from the sun. In a large number of homes, solar energy provides hot water.

The solar panels on this house capture energy from the sun. That solar energy is converted to heat energy, which warms the air and water.

Design and build a model solar home and/or a model solar collector for heating hot water.

MICROCLIMATES

Is the temperature in one room of a house the same as the temperature throughout the house? Does the furniture in a house affect the *microclimates*—the temperature areas of a room? Is a cup of coffee as hot at the top as at the bottom? Does the shape of a coffee cup (tall and skinny or short and wide) affect the way heat is distributed inside the cup? Using temperature probes and a computer, you can easily find out. You may need the probes with the 50-foot leads for experiments in a room.

Do your findings have any bearing on the design of heating vents, windows, and furniture placement for an energy-efficient home?

CHAPTER 7

Electricity

In 1791, Luigi Galvani found that connecting two different metals could make a frog's muscle contract just as surely as the spark created by a Leyden jar, an apparatus that stores electricity. About 10 years later, Alessandro Volta found that the electricity produced was the result of the two different metals and had nothing to do with the frog.

A pile of metal disks arranged in the order of zinc-copper-zinc-copper with cardboard disks moistened in saltwater between the metals resulted in a continuous flow of electricity when the top and bottom of the pile were connected with a wire. Volta had invented the first electric battery.

In 1831, Michael Faraday showed that electricity can be produced by changing the magnetic field through a coil of wire. This is the principle used to produce electricity in modern power plants. A large coil of wire turns in a magnetic field. The work required to turn the wire is supplied by moving water or steam that comes from water heated by burning coal, oil, gas, or from heat supplied by a nuclear reactor. Unlike a battery, in which the chemicals that supply the electricity are eventually used up, an electric generator will continue to produce electricity as long as the coil turns in the magnetic field.

Electrical experiments can be dangerous, so keep the following safety tips in mind. Do not use household current when dry cells or batteries are specified. You might be electrocuted. Make sure wires of components don't burn you or get so hot that they start a fire.

BENDING WATER WITH ELECTRICITY

On a day when the humidity is low, rub a hard rubber rod or plastic comb or ruler on some woolen clothing to give it a negative charge. Then bring the rod near a thin stream of water flowing from a faucet. You'll see the water bend toward the rod.

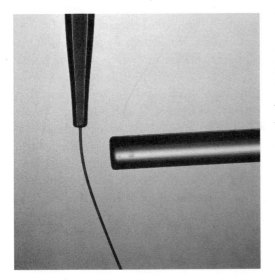

When a negatively charged rod is placed next to a stream of water flowing from a faucet, the water bends.

What kinds of objects, when rubbed with wool, will produce this effect? Glass rods? Balloons? Other things? Can you get a similar effect if you rub the rod on a material other than wool? How about paper? If you change the sign of the charge by using a glass rod instead of rubber, will the water be repelled by, instead of attracted to, the rod?

Will other liquid streams show a similar effect when near an electrically charged rod? *Avoid using flammable liquids such as alcohol. A highly charged rod might cause a spark that could ignite the liquid.*

TESTING CONDUCTORS AND INSULATORS

Solids and liquids through which electricity flows easily are called *conductors*; materials that do not allow electricity to flow through them are called *insulators*.

You can test different solids and liquids to see if they conduct electricity by placing them in series with a flashlight bulb. Set up the circuit shown in Figure 17. Connect the leads between the battery and the bulb to the ends of a solid you want to test. Test a variety of items such as silverware, nails, plastic, pencils, wood, and paper. If the bulb lights, the solid is a conductor. Which solids are conductors? What do you know about the solid in the circuit if the bulb doesn't light?

To test the conductivity of liquids, slide two paper clips over the edge of a medicine cup filled with the liquid you want to test, as shown in Figure 18 on page 94. At least the lower half of both paper clips should be in the liquid. Connect the two leads to the paper clip and see if the bulb lights.

Test such liquids as water, milk, lemon juice, saturated solutions of salt, sugar, and baking soda. Which are conductors? Repeat your tests for the liquids that appear to be nonconductors. In some of these liquids, you may find gas bubbling up around the paper clips even though the bulb doesn't light. What does this suggest?

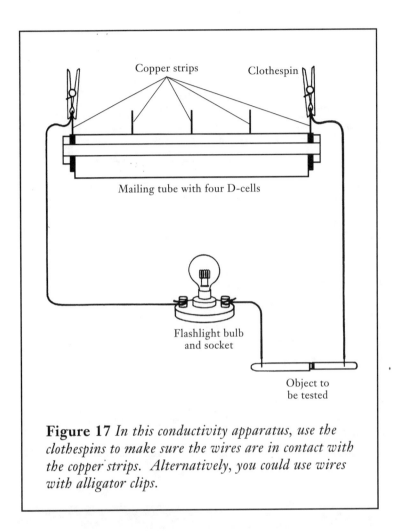

Figure 17 *In this conductivity apparatus, use the clothespins to make sure the wires are in contact with the copper strips. Alternatively, you could use wires with alligator clips.*

You might get more precise in this experiment by testing how conductive a substance is. Using an *ohm* meter, or the ohm scale on a battery-powered Volt-Ohm-Current meter (available from an electronics or hardware store), or a conductivity probe hooked to a computer, find the resistance, in ohms, of different conductors. What are semiconductors?

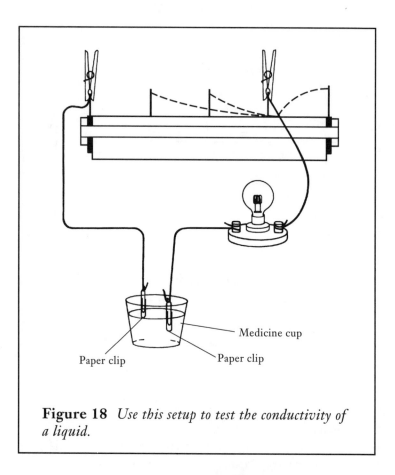

Figure 18 *Use this setup to test the conductivity of a liquid.*

Medicine cup

Paper clip

Paper clip

ELECTRICITY FROM FRUIT AND NAILS

Volta used two different metals and a salt solution to produce electricity. The batteries, or electrical cells (D cells, C cells, etc.) that you buy today also consist of two metals immersed in an electrolyte (something that will conduct electricity). You can make some simple electric cells using two metals and a variety of fruits and vegetables as electrolytes.

Gather a number of different fruits and vegetables, such as

a lemon, an apple, an orange, a potato, a pickle, and a couple of olives. You'll also need a sensitive galvanometer or microammeter or computer current/voltage probes, wire leads, paper towels, water, and nails or strips made from several different metals such as copper, aluminum, iron, zinc, and nickel.

Shine the metals with steel wool. Clean them this way each time you use them.

Connect one end of each of two wire leads to two poles (+ and –) of the meter. Then put the nails into one of the fruits or vegetables. Do you have any evidence that electricity is produced? Can you get the meter needle to move backward (left instead of right)? If the needle does move to the right, what happens if you switch the metals so that their leads to the meter are reversed? Does the electric current measured on the meter depend on how far apart the nails are? Does it depend on how deeply the nails are pushed into the fruit? Does it depend on which nails are used? Does it depend on which fruit or vegetable is used? Which fruit seems to be the best electrolyte?

Can you get a current to flow if you squeeze two different metals in your fingers? If you touch the metals to your skin? Are you a conductor of electricity?

As you have seen, to make the meter needle move to the right, one metal of a particular combination must be connected to the + lead of the meter. Sometimes, to make the needle move right, the metal connected to the + lead must be connected to the – lead when paired with a different metal. With that in mind, try to establish which of the metals is the most positive metal. Which is the most negative? Using a small digital clock (that you can hang up with Velcro) with a dead battery, hook up the leads to your vegetable battery. Does it work? Is a digital potato clock very accurate?

BUILD A BETTER BATTERY

Now that you've built some simple batteries, read some books and articles about batteries. On the basis of your research, build your own Daniell cell. Build a model lead storage cell. What are the advantages of a lead storage cell over a Daniell cell?

The success of the electric car depends on the development of a battery that can be recharged thousands of times. See if you can make such a battery.

RESISTING ELECTRICITY

The electrical resistance of a circuit element—a bulb, wire, motor, or whatever—is defined as the ratio of the potential difference (voltmeter reading) across the element to the current through the element for a given temperature. With a circuit like the one in Figure 19, you can measure the resistance of any circuit element. Note that the voltmeter is wired in parallel (side-by-side branches) with the element, while the ammeter is in series (one after the other). The battery consists of eight D cells in series.

Measure the resistance of some small resistors. To be sure they don't burn out, and to maintain a nearly constant temperature, place the resistors in a small amount of water. Measure the current and voltage as you increase the size of the battery from one cell to eight. Plot a graph of voltage versus current (or use a computer with voltage/current probes and have the program plot the graph for you every second). Is the ratio constant? How can you tell? You can also measure the resistance of a number of other circuit elements: small DC electric motors, flashlight bulbs, and various long pieces of wire such as the ones used to replace the heating elements in electric stoves.

How is the resistance of a wire related to its length? How does the resistance of the wire filament in a flashlight bulb change as the wire gets hotter?

What is the resistance of your voltmeter? Of your ammeter? Of a D cell? Of a vacuum tube? Measure the resistance of each of two resistors. Connect them in series; then connect them in parallel. What happens to the total resistance when they are wired in series? When they're wired in parallel? How do you think the resistance of a wire is related to its cross-sectional area? Find a way to test your prediction. Were you right?

Connect two of your fingers to conductivity probes

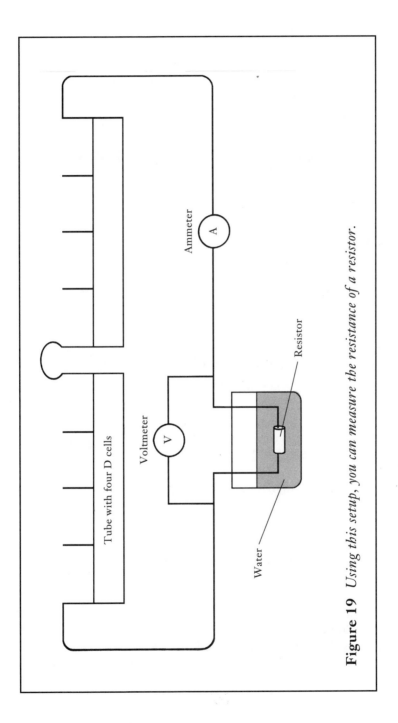

Figure 19 *Using this setup, you can measure the resistance of a resistor.*

Tube with four D cells

Ammeter

Voltmeter

Resistor

Water

hooked to a computer and measure your own resistance. Now think of something really frightening and see what happens. Think of something really happy and check again. Could you construct an "emotion meter"? What do "lie detectors" (or "polygraphs") test?

A POSSIBLE SURPRISE

With a flashlight bulb, a socket, a D cell, and some wire leads, you can make a simple circuit that contains a glowing bulb. What do you think will happen if you lower the bulb into a glass of water? Try it. Were you surprised? How can you explain the result? If you have difficulty, think about the electrical resistance of water compared to metal wires. Can you predict the result if you repeat the experiment using saltwater instead of plain water?

ENERGY AND ELECTRIC CHARGE

Does the energy supplied by a flow of charge depend on the quantity of charge?

To find out, heat some water in a calorimeter by letting a known amount of electric charge flow through a wire immersed in water. The heating wire can be a short piece of a heating element coil used to repair electric stoves, or you can use a piece of nichrome wire. In either case, the wire should have a resistance of about 2 ohms.

Since electric current is the rate of charge flow, the total charge that flows (measured in ampere-seconds) is equal to current (in amperes) times time (in seconds):

$$\text{Charge} = \text{current} \times \text{time}$$

After recording the initial temperature with a thermometer that can read temperature to the nearest 0.1°C, let a current of 4 amps flow through the wire immersed in 100 g of water, as shown in Figure 20 (use a low-voltage variable power supply).

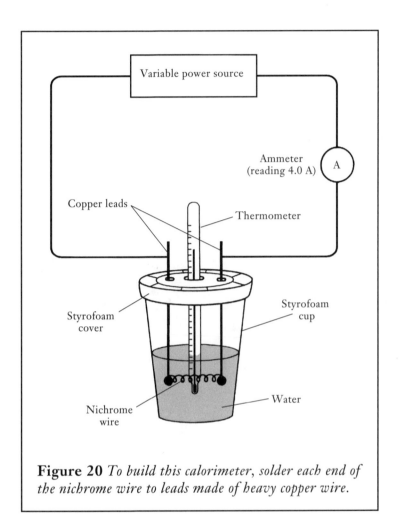

Figure 20 *To build this calorimeter, solder each end of the nichrome wire to leads made of heavy copper wire.*

After 30 seconds, turn off the current, gently stir the water to be sure the heat is evenly distributed, and record the maximum temperature. A computer temperature probe can give you a continuous graph and record your readings every second.

Repeat the experiment using another 100 g of cool water. This time let the 4-amp current run for 60 seconds. Make two more runs for 90- and 120-second intervals. Why should you start each run with cool water?

What's the relationship between the heat delivered and the quantity of charge? What's the relationship between the heat per charge and the charge when a constant current flows for different periods of time? How could you reduce the errors in this experiment?

THE DIRECTION OF CHARGE FLOW

Using your knowledge of electricity, design experiments to show that electric charge flows in only one direction along wires but in two directions within electric cells and electrolytic solutions.

WHAT DOES A VOLTMETER MEASURE?

A voltmeter measures voltage, or better, potential difference. But what does that mean? Here's a way to find out.

Connect a voltmeter to the apparatus shown in Figure 20. After recording the temperature of 100 g of water to the nearest 0.1°C, allow a current of 4 amps to flow for 60 seconds. Record the voltmeter reading, current, time, and change in temperature. Since you know that less charge will reduce the heat delivered, you should increase the time as you reduce the current and voltage in succeeding runs. Therefore, in the next run let a current of 3 amps flow for 120 seconds, then 2 amps for 3 minutes, and, finally, 1 amp for 4 minutes.

Calculate the heat delivered in calories and the charge in ampere-seconds for each run. Then plot a graph of *heat per charge* on the vertical axis versus voltage across the heater. What do you find? What does a voltmeter measure? Write an equation relating heat, current, time, and voltage.

The product (voltage × current × time) is measured in *joules*. If you measure heat in joules, write an equation relating heat, current, time, and voltage. How many joules are equivalent to 1 calorie?

GENERATING ELECTRICITY

Faraday found that he could generate electricity by changing the magnetic field within a coil of wire. You can duplicate Faraday's feat by moving a bar magnet in and out of a coil of wire connected to a microammeter or galvanometer, as shown in Figure 21.

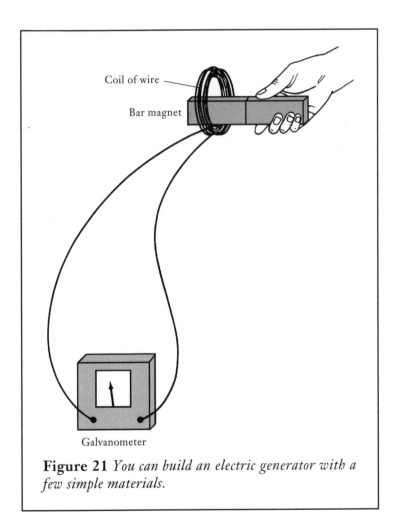

Coil of wire

Bar magnet

Galvanometer

Figure 21 *You can build an electric generator with a few simple materials.*

The amount of electricity generated in this simple demonstration is small, and you would quickly tire of moving the magnet. Can you build a generator that will generate enough electricity to light a flashlight bulb? One that will run continuously without the use of "muscle power"?

The Duracell Company, which makes batteries, holds a contest each year for the best project or device built by a student using at least one battery. Ask your science teacher about the contest to see if you can compete with one of your inventions, or contact the company at: Duracell, Chicago, IL 60645 or (312) 262-6916 or http://www.duracellcom.com. You can also find information about the contest at http://smec.uncwil.edu/resrcs/stucomp.htm. A particularly good site for finding out about 300 contests for high-school students is http://www.intraweb.com/aet.html.

CHAPTER 8

Body-and-Mind Science

Human physiology is the study of the life processes that go on within our bodies. Psychology is the science of mental processes, the activities that go on within our brain. Most people enjoy these subject areas because they're really studying themselves.

Caution: This chapter includes experiments that should be performed only on people who are healthy and in normal physical condition. If you're thinking of entering one of these projects in a science fair, check the rules to be sure that projects involving humans are allowed.

HOW TIME FLIES

Without looking at a watch, can you tell when 1 minute has passed? How about 5 minutes? 1 hour? Does time seem to slow down when you are bored and speed up when you're busy? Does time seem to pass faster as you get older?

How good are you at estimating time? When the second hand of a clock reaches 12, turn away. Try not to count seconds, but when you think a minute has passed, look at the clock again. Was your guess a short minute or a long one?

Now, try to guess when 5 minutes have passed; then, when 10 have passed. Try to estimate 30 minutes. Are you less accurate at estimating longer periods than shorter ones?

Try estimating how much time has passed while you read different things, such as a novel or a page in a dictionary. Does the kind of material you're reading affect the way you estimate time? Estimate time as you listen to different types of music. Does fast music make time seem to pass faster than slow music? Finally, try to estimate time while you're doing physically active things, such as running, cycling, or doing household chores.

Once you've studied your own ability to estimate time and how your estimates are affected by various factors, try the same experiments on other people. Try to find subjects of both genders and of various ages. Work with each person individually and keep a record of his or her estimates. Record whether the guesses are too long or too short by writing the error as, for example, +12 seconds or –8 seconds. Also record the individual's name, age, and sex as well as the date of the experiment.

Computer software such as Vernier Software's *Precision Timer* will change any computer into a recording stopwatch. Your subject doesn't have to see the screen, just press a spacebar, mouse button, or joystick button to start and stop the time interval. The computer will record all the responses, put them in a data table, and graph the results. With your data, you can calculate the standard deviation and other useful statistics (see Appendix 2) to determine whether your results are "statistically significant."

Use your results to look for patterns. Do elderly people tend to overestimate time that has passed? Do females estimate time better than males? Does season affect estimates?

LOOKS CAN BE DECEIVING

Look at the optical illusions in Figure 22. Things we see can often deceive our brain. Look at the moon as it rises and ascends into the sky. Is it really larger on the horizon? Look at the rising moon with your chin on your chest so that you view it through the upper part of your visual field. Does this change its apparent size? Try to explain this lunar illusion.

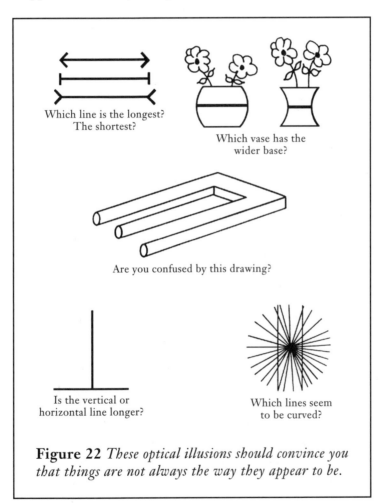

Which line is the longest? The shortest?

Which vase has the wider base?

Are you confused by this drawing?

Is the vertical or horizontal line longer?

Which lines seem to be curved?

Figure 22 *These optical illusions should convince you that things are not always the way they appear to be.*

Design some illusions of your own. Test them on other people and see if you can explain why they create the effects they do.

TO SLEEP PERCHANCE TO DREAM

Do you move in your sleep? Do you dream? It's likely that we all dream, but many of us don't remember our dreams. Next time you go to sleep, try to remember the last position you were in before you dozed off. Are you in the same position when you wake up? Watch your friends or family members (with their permission, of course) as they sleep. Do they move? Do they talk? Do their eyes move?

You can detect a person's eye movements even if their eyes are closed. Rapid back-and-forth eye movement during sleep is called REM sleep. REM stands for "rapid eye movement." It's during REM sleep that most people dream. If you can watch someone who claims not to dream, you'll find that the individual goes through periods of REM sleep about four to six times each night. If you wake the person during REM sleep, they will probably recall what they were dreaming.

If you're a person who doesn't remember dreams, try this for several mornings. Set your alarm clock to awaken you half an hour earlier than usual. There's a good chance that you'll be in REM sleep—and hence dreaming. Most people pass through REM sleep shortly before they wake.

You may also be able to remember your dreams if, when you first awaken, you pay attention to the first thing that comes to mind. Chances are it may have something to do with the last dream you had before waking, and this may lead you to remember the entire dream.

Keep a record of your dreams. Do you dream about the things you think about or do during the day? Do you often have the same or similar dreams? If you're awakened, can you go back to sleep and finish a dream? Do you ever solve problems while you're asleep? Many people do. What evidence do you have that animals dream? Do dogs and cats have REM sleep?

ARE YOU IN SHAPE?

Here's a way to determine if someone is in good physical condition. It's called the Harvard step test. Simply have the subject step up onto and down from a bench or step thirty times per minute for 4 minutes. The height of the bench should be related to the height of the individual as shown in Table 3.

TABLE 3 RELATIONSHIP BETWEEN BENCH HEIGHT AND SUBJECT HEIGHT

Height of bench (inches)	Height of subject (feet, inches)
12	Less than 5'0"
14	5'0" to 5'3"
16	5'4" to 5'9"
18	5'10" to 6'0"
20	More than 6'0"

After the subject has completed the test, wait 1 minute. Then count his or her heartbeats for 30 seconds. Two minutes after the exercise, again count the number of heartbeats in 30 seconds. Do the same 3 minutes after the exercise.

From the data collected, calculate the recovery index (RI) according to the formula:.

$$RI = \frac{\text{Duration of exercise in seconds} \times 100}{\text{Sum of heartbeats} \times 2}$$

Suppose you collect the following data on a subject:

Time after exercise (minutes)	Number of heartbeats
1 to 1.5	50
2 to 2.5	45
3 to 3.5	40

The RI would be calculated as follows:

$$RI = \frac{240 \times 100}{(50 + 45 + 40) \times 2} = \frac{24{,}000}{135 \times 2} = \frac{24{,}000}{270} = 89$$

The relationship between your subject's physical condition and the recovery index is shown in Table 4.

Test a number of subjects. Are athletes in better shape than nonathletes? Are distance runners in better condition than other athletes? Can you detect those who smoke?

See if you can devise a better test for physical condition. You might include breathing rate as well as heart rate, and find the time required for the subject to return to the same heart rate, as well as the time required to return to the same heart and breathing rates that existed before the exercise. Maybe the coaches at your school would be interested in using your test.

If you have access to a computer with special probes or instruments, you can conduct an interesting follow-up to this experiment. For example, Vernier Software makes a Heart Rate Monitor, a Respiration Monitor Belt (to measure breathing rate), an EKG electrode set (to show the heart's electrical signals), a temperature probe set (to measure skin temperature changes), and an Electrical Conductivity Probe (to determine skin conductivity).

Using any or all of these, you can develop a comprehensive profile of the effects of exercise on your volunteers. You can record every heartbeat instead of counting for 15 seconds and then multiplying by four. You can record the changes in heart rate

TABLE 4   DETERMINING PHYSICAL CONDITION

Physical condition	Recovery index
Poor	Less than 50
Fair	51 to 65
Good	66 to 80
Excellent	More than 80

in a table and get an instant graph of what is happening. With a computer and these probes, you can get much more information than the best physicians were able to get just a few years ago.

REACTION TIME

Here's a safe bet. Tell your friend she can keep a dollar bill if she can catch it before it falls through her fingers after you release it. A paper dollar is about 6 inches (15 cm) long. If your friend holds her fingers 2 inches (5 cm) from the bottom of the bill, she must react before the dollar falls 4 inches (10 cm); that is, within 0.15 second. Few people have such a fast reaction time.

To measure someone's reaction time, have that person place her fingers around the very bottom of a smooth yardstick that you hold in a vertical position. Tell the subject to catch the yardstick between her fingers as soon as it begins to fall. The person should not try to anticipate when you're going to release the yardstick. Check the chart below to determine the person's reaction time. Can you make a similar chart for reaction time in terms of centimeters that a meter stick falls before being caught?

Suppose you collect the following data on a subject:

Distance yardstick falls before it is caught (inches)	Reaction time (second)
6	0.18
12	0.25
18	0.31
24	0.35
30	0.40
36	0.43

Test a number of people. Do you find any patterns? Do girls react faster than boys of the same age? Does reaction time change with age? Are athletes faster than nonathletes? Are people whose work requires exceptional manual dexterity, such as surgeons or artists, faster than others? What else do you find? How were the reaction times in the chart established?

Try to invent a better method for measuring reaction time. Would a computer program such as *Precision Timer* measure reaction times accurately?

HOW POWERFUL ARE YOU?

Can you work like a horse? You may be surprised to find that you can.

If you walk up a flight of stairs, you do some work on yourself. If you run up the stairs, you do the same amount of work but in a shorter time. The rate at which work is done is called *power*.

$$Power = Work/time$$

Power can be measured in foot•pounds per second, joules per second (watts), or any units of force × distance (work) divided by time. A common unit of power that you've probably heard of is *horsepower*. One horsepower is 550 footpounds of work per second, or 746 watts (Joules per second).

To determine how much power you can develop, have someone measure the time it takes you to run up a long flight of stairs. To calculate your power, you need to know the vertical height of the stairs, your weight, and the time it took you to ascend the stairs. The product of your weight and the height of the stairs is the work you did on yourself. If you divide that work done by the time to do it, you will find your power.

$$P = \frac{w \times h}{t}$$

where P is power, w is weight, h is height, and t is time.

For example, if you weigh 120 pounds (54 kg) and run up a flight of stairs 12 feet (4 m) high in 4 seconds, your power can be calculated as shown below:

$$P = \frac{120 \text{ lb} \times 12 \text{ ft}}{4 \text{ sec}} = 360 \text{ ft•lb/sec} = 0.66 \text{ hp}$$

This man is flexing the large biceps in his upper arm. This muscle is usually developed by doing arm curling exercises.

Try it! How powerful are you?

Use the same method to find how much horsepower other people can develop. What do you find? Is the power that a person can develop related to age? Gender? Height? Weight?

Suppose you measure the power developed over a greater height—five flights of stairs instead of one or two. How does this affect an individual's ability to develop power? Can you explain why? Using a spreadsheet to record your data will allow you to make calculations instantly as you enter new figures, graph power as a function of age, height, or weight, and do statistical analyses of your data to see if the differences are "significant."

MUSCLE PAIRS

Muscles can do work only when contracting. That's why most muscles come in pairs. Your biceps enable you to bend your forearm toward your shoulder; your triceps are used to straighten or extend your arm. Usually one muscle of a pair is stronger than the other. That's why you can kick harder in a forward direction than in a backward direction.

You can use a bathroom scale to measure the strength of some muscle pairs. Sit on a chair and push your foot forward against a scale that is resting against a wall. How hard can you push forward? Now stand the scale on end against one leg of the chair you're sitting on. Use the other member of the muscle pair to press your heel against the scale. How hard can your muscles push backward?

Use the same scale or a spring scale to measure the relative strength of other paired muscles. You may want a helper to hold the scale or read it. Look for muscle pairs that move parts of your body in opposite directions. You've already heard of the muscles that flex and extend the lower arm. Similarly, there are muscle pairs that push fingers apart or squeeze them together; muscles that push your toes down or lift them up; muscles that allow you to move your head forward and back. What other muscle pairs can you find? Is one member of a muscle pair always much stronger than the other? Can you increase the strength of the weaker muscle through exercise, or will the ratio of the relative strengths of the pair remain constant? What's your strongest muscle?

Compare your muscle strengths with those of other people. Do any have muscle pairs in which the strongest muscle is the opposite of yours? Is the relative strength of paired muscles related to the work or exercise that people do?

Once you've established a good method to determine strengths and have standardized your tests for a group of individuals, try changing their environment. Do your subjects produce more force in a cold room or in a hot room? Are they stronger with rock music, classical music, country-western, or some other type of music? Do other sounds, lighting, or humidity make a difference? Make sure you use good controls and calculate statistics to see if the differences in your data are significant.

MUSCLE FATIGUE

You know that muscles tire with use. To see how much strength your finger muscles lose through use, hold a bathroom scale with one hand on either side. Squeeze as hard as you can. With what force can you squeeze the scale? Put the scale down and open and close your fingers as fast as you can for 1 minute. Then immediately squeeze the scale again. Have you gained or lost strength in your fingers? How much? How long does it take before your strength is the same as before?

Do the muscles of people stronger than you tire more or less than yours? How about the muscles of people weaker than you?

BODY FACTS

It's easy to find a person's height, weight, and age, but what really counts in terms of shedding excess heat or estimating body fat percentages are the body's surface area, volume, and density. Develop methods that enable you to determine the surface area, volume, and density of a person's body.

How does a person's strength vary with height and weight? Unless you have a very large sample of people to work with, you may have to consult tables from an Internet source or physiology textbook. Use *Graphical Analysis* to see how strength varies with weight and height.

CHAPTER 9

Plant
Science

When you think of plants, you probably have visions of green trees and pretty flowers, but plants come in many shapes and sizes. Green plants provide us with the food and oxygen we need for life.

DECOMPOSITION RATES

Gather a few handfuls of tree leaves. What can you do to increase the rate at which these leaves decompose? What can you do to decrease the natural decomposition rate of the leaves? What advice could you give to composters?

Compost piles get warm. How warm? Does the temperature vary during the day and/or night? Temperature probes on long leads can help you record and graph the temperature inside the compost pile compared to the temperature outside. Can you determine the heat produced by a specific amount of compost per unit of time?

SEED DISPERSAL

Seeds are distributed in various ways. Some seeds are dispersed by the wind. Others are spread by animals or water.

Collect seeds and/or fruit from as many plants as possible. See if you can determine how each plant disperses its seeds. What special mechanisms for dispersal can you find? Are some seeds dispersed in more than one way?

For seeds that are distributed by the wind, set up an experiment to see how long it takes a seed with wings or fluff to travel a specific distance. Record seed heights on trees and wind speeds in a spreadsheet table to determine the widest possible distribution from a particular type of tree.

BLOOMING WILDFLOWERS

In the spring, summer, and fall, open fields are often filled with colorful wildflowers. If you look at these flowers carefully, you'll see that as temperature, length of day, rainfall, and other conditions change, so do the species of wildflowers that bloom.

Does the height of the flowers in bloom change with the season? Are the flowers that bloom in May as tall as those that blossom in September?

In a field or park in mid-May, find as many blooming wildflowers as you can. Measure the height of the blossom above the ground for at least ten specimens of each species. Take an average of all your measurements to get a value for the average blossom height in May. If possible, collect, dry, and preserve a sample of each species. (Ask a biology teacher the best way to do this.) Repeat this experiment each month until autumn's cold brings blooming to an end.

A bar graph of your results may help you see if the average height of flowers is related to the time of year. (Again, recording your information in a spreadsheet makes graphing very easy.) Does the average height of wildflowers change as the year progresses from spring to fall? If you find a pattern, can you offer an explanation?

In most parts of the United States, daisies bloom in the late spring and early summer.

SEPARATING PLANT PIGMENTS

You know that leaves contain colored pigments. After all, most leaves are green, but turn other colors in autumn. To separate the pigments in leaves you can use a technique called paper chromatography. ***This project involves chemicals. Work in a well-ventilated area and wear your safety goggles.***

Collect a variety of leaves. While the leaves are still fresh, cut strips of filter paper about about $\frac{3}{4}$ inch × 4 inches (2 cm × 10 cm). To transfer the pigment to the paper strips, place a leaf on the paper about $\frac{3}{4}$ inch (2 cm) from one end. Roll the edge of a coin or washer over the leaf to crush the leaf tissue. Repeat the process several times, each time using a fresh part of the leaf over the same place on the paper. You can also extract pigments using a food processor, blender, or even a mortar and pestle with sand in it to grind the leaves. Use a medicine dropper to apply the juice to the filter paper. Prepare one strip for each type of leaf you collected.

After the leaf tissue on the paper has dried, use tape to hang the strips in groups of two or three from a pencil or stick. The pigmented stripe should be on the bottom. Lower each set of paper strips into a beaker that contains enough acetone (or non-oily fingernail polish remover, which is mostly acetone) to almost reach the bottom of the strips (the acetone should be below the strip of crushed leaf tissue). *Handle acetone with care. It is flammable and toxic. Cover the beakers to avoid breathing in the vapors.*

The pencil will support the strips and allow you to watch the ascending acetone carry different pigments to various heights along the paper. You may want to change the length of the paper strips to get better separation of pigments.

Let the strips dry. Then look at the pigments that have been separated. Which leaf contained the most pigments? Place each dry paper strip next to the leaf from which the colors came to make an interesting display.

Can grain, wood, or rubbing alcohol be used to separate pigments? If they can, is there a difference in how far one band of color moves compared to another in different solvents?

EXPERIMENT WITH SEEDS AND SEEDLINGS

You can investigate a number of factors that influence seed and seedling growth using bean or corn seeds; plastic, cardboard, or other containers; and vermiculite or soil for the seeds to grow in.

To begin, you might try to find out if seeds will germinate underwater, or whether seeds need any water at all to germinate. Do deeply planted seeds grow better than those planted close to the surface? Will seeds germinate in the dark? Will seedlings grow in darkness? If they will, how does their growth compare with that of seedlings grown in light? Can you predict what will happen if you cover the leaves of a seedling growing in light? Will seeds kept in a freezer germinate? Will seedlings left in a freezer overnight continue to grow? Over what temperature range can seedlings grow? Will seedlings grow in saltwater?

Can a seedling germinate if you cut off its root? If you cut off its leaves? If you cut off what remains of the seed after it has germinated?

Place a growing plant near a window. Does it bend toward the light? If it does, what happens when you turn it around? Does its direction of growth change again? If it does, how long does it take to change? Does the color of the light affect the direction of a plant's growth? Do plants grow better in light of a particular color? Suitable filters can be obtained from a photography store. Freestyle Photo Sales of Los Angeles (address in Chapter 3) sells filters for bulbs.

Plant some seeds in a clear plastic container so that you can watch as they germinate. Which way do the roots grow? Which way do the stems grow? Once the seeds have germinated, turn the box on its side. What happens to the direction of growth of the roots and stems now? Can you use light to make stems grow down instead of up?

Put a sheet of cardboard on an old phonograph turntable. Fasten a container of seedlings growing in vermiculite to the cardboard. Be sure the weight is evenly distributed along the diameter of the turntable. Let the seedlings rotate for several days. What happens? How do they compare with a control group? Is there a significant difference? Use a spreadsheet and statistical analysis techniques to find out if the differences are significant(see Appendixes 2 and 3).

Does the rate of rotation affect the direction of growth? Does the distance of the seedlings from the center of the turntable have an effect? What happens to the growth pattern after the seedlings stop rotating? If you have trouble understanding the results of your rotating-plant experiments, read some books that discuss ways of creating an artificial gravity in space.

Let some seedlings grow in soil until they flower and produce their own seeds. When the seeds dry, collect them. Plant some of the seeds right away. Store others for several months before planting. Store some in a freezer, some in a refrigerator, some in a warm place, and the rest at room temperature—half in darkness and half in light. Do all the seeds germinate? What conditions seem to be the best for storing seeds? Is this true of all types of seeds? Again, the differences in germination must be significant for you to make firm conclusions.

CLONING PLANTS

Cloning means the reproduction of genetically identical organisms. This is difficult to do in higher animals, but some plants can be cloned with a cutting from an existing plant. One common method is called rooting.

To clone plants, first build a "bed" for rooting. Punch some good-sized holes in the bottom of a plastic container (an old dishpan works well) with a large nail. The holes will allow excess moisture to drain away and prevent the plants from rotting. Put a piece of paper towel or facial tissue over each hole and pour in sand or vermiculite to a depth of about 6 inches (15 cm). Add water to moisten the rooting bed.

Start with a coleus plant, which is easy to root. Use a sharp knife to cut off a plant about 2 inches (5 cm) above the soil. Will the plant that has been cut off continue to grow, generating a new stem and leaves? Trim off the lower leaves of the plant you have cut away and stick the stem into the rooting bed. Make several similar cuttings.

Use coat-hanger wire and plastic sheeting to build a greenhouse that covers the bed like the one shown in Figure 23. Place the bed in an area that receives light but not direct sunlight. Lift the plastic and feel the soil every day. If it feels dry, add rainwater or tapwater that has been allowed to sit for several days so that chlorine can escape.

After two weeks, reach under the plastic and give each plant a gentle tug. If it moves easily, leave it for another week, but if it seems to be firmly implanted, dig around the plant and remove it. Has the plant grown new roots?

Using this method, try rooting other plants such as chrysanthemums, philodendrons, ivies, African violets, begonias, and geraniums. Will some of these plants root if you use a single leaf? Can you get a bean plant to root? Cut the stem of a bean plant about 3 inches (8 cm) below the *cotyledon* leaf remains and

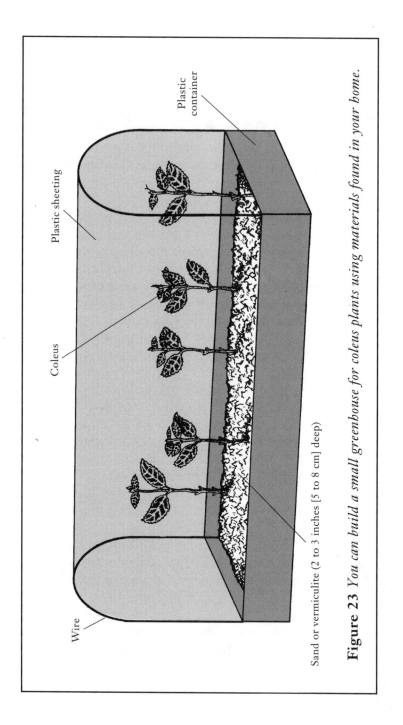

Figure 23 *You can build a small greenhouse for coleus plants using materials found in your home.*

Plastic container

Plastic sheeting

Coleus

Wire

Sand or vermiculite (2 to 3 inches [5 to 8 cm] deep)

place it in the rooting bed. Will it take root? Will the old root and remaining stem regenerate a new plant? Design an experiment to find out how temperature affects the rooting process.

There are substances that are supposed to speed up the rooting process in plants. Buy some at a florist's or garden store and design experiments to see if they really work. To see if other chemicals will induce rooting, trim some bean plants as shown in Figure 24. Place them in pint containers of water and other chemicals.

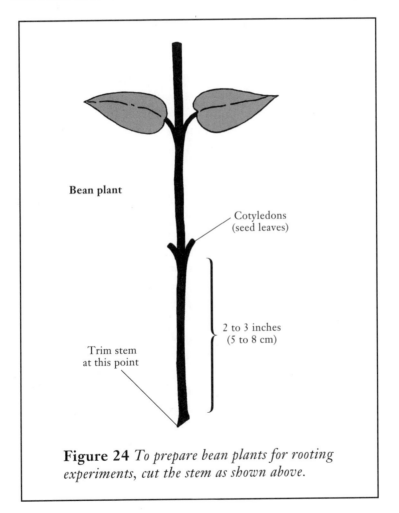

Bean plant

Cotyledons
(seed leaves)

2 to 3 inches
(5 to 8 cm)

Trim stem
at this point

Figure 24 *To prepare bean plants for rooting experiments, cut the stem as shown above.*

Prepare a boric acid solution by adding a teaspoonful of the white powder to a gallon of water. Put a teaspoonful of the solution into a 1-pint container of water with bean cuttings. Observe the plants over several weeks. Try different concentrations of boric acid as well as salt, sugar, baking soda, and special rooting chemicals. How do these various chemicals affect the rooting?

PHOTOSYNTHESIS AND LIGHT

The world's green plants can "capture" light and store it as chemical energy in the food they manufacture. The process by which they manufacture food is called *photosynthesis*. During photosynthesis, green plants use the light from the sun to convert carbon dioxide and water into food and oxygen. The food contains more energy than the water and carbon dioxide from which it was made. The added energy comes from sunlight.

The oxygen formed during photosynthesis is the gas we breathe. Since only green plants carry on this marvelous process, the earth's entire source of food and oxygen comes from green plants. Without them, life as we know it would be impossible.

Do plants that don't look green, such as the deep-purple leaves of the Japanese plum, contain chlorophyll? Or do they use some other pigment? Can you use your chromatography tests to find out?

To see that light is essential for food production in green plants, you can test some leaves that have been in light and compare them with leaves that have been in the dark before testing. The test consists of finding out whether there is starch (food) in the leaf tissue.

Prepare some *Lugol's solution* by dissolving 5 g of iodine and 10 g of potassium iodide crystals in 100 ml of water. ***Don't forget your safety goggles.*** Add a drop or two of the solution to a suspension of starch in water. The dark-blue color produced when iodine reacts with starch serves as a test for starch.

Completely cover one leaf on a geranium plant with black

paper. Use paper clips to hold the paper in place. Cover another leaf with a piece of black paper that has a circular hole in it. Expose the plant to a bright light for 24 hours. Remove the two leaves that were totally or partially covered as well as one leaf that was exposed to light. Break the cell walls in these leaves by placing the leaves in boiling water.

Once the leaves are limp, you can extract the chlorophyll from the leaves by placing them in hot alcohol. *Do not heat alcohol with an open flame. Put the alcohol in a small beaker, which can be placed in a larger beaker that contains water. Heat the water on an electric hot plate.* You will see the leaves grow pale as their chlorophyll dissolves in alcohol. When the leaves are quite pale, remove them with forceps and put them one at a time into a shallow bath of Lugol's solution. If starch, which is not soluble in alcohol, is present, the leaves turn dark-blue. What evidence do you have to indicate that light is essential for photosynthesis?

Design an experiment to show that carbon dioxide is required for photosynthesis. Design one to detect the release of oxygen during this process.

CHAPTER 10

Animal Science

There are a great variety of animals on earth. You can't possibly investigate all of them, but these projects should allow you to study some of them.

Treat mammals, fish, and insects with respect. Observe or collect so that you disrupt their lives as little as possible. Try to release all specimens where you found them. Check science fair guidelines for special restrictions on animal projects.

SPYING ON BIRDS

With a field guide to help you, you can begin to study the birds that live in your area. A pair of binoculars will allow you to view birds more closely, but they are not essential. Use a notebook to record all the birds you see, where you see them, when you see them, and what they are doing.

When you find a bird that you haven't identified, ask yourself these questions: How big is it compared to birds you already know? What shape does it have? Is it chunky or slender? Is its bill long or short? Is its head crested? How does it move? Does it fly in straight lines, weave up and down, dart to and fro, or soar? On the ground, does it walk or hop? Or is it a waterbird that glides along the water's surface? What are its markings? Its colors? Does it sing a characteristic song? Take a tape recorder with you to record its songs. What does it eat? What does it feed its young? What are its eggs like? Do both males and females care for the young?

If you have a computer with a CD-ROM drive, you can get disks that will have color pictures of each bird and will play their songs. A video recorder with a telephoto lens will help you to identify the birds later.

Once you've learned to identify the birds where you live, study them in a more scientific way. How can nests be used to identify birds? How do birds build them? Where do they build them? What do they eat? Which migrating bird returns first in the spring? Do both sexes return together, or does one precede the other? Which species stay through the winter? Make a sample count of each species from time to time. Does the relative number of each species change from season to season or even from week to week?

Build or buy a bird feeder. Put it in a sheltered place where you can observe the birds that come to feed. Try out different foods. Which birds are attracted to grains of wheat or corn? Which ones like fat trimmings or suet? Do any like peanut butter or jelly? Using food coloring, color sunflower seeds with different colors. Do birds seem to be attracted to—or repelled by—particular colors?

Do some birds chase other birds away? Do some birds carry the food away rather than feasting at the feeder? Which birds dart in for a quick bite and then leave? Which ones stay for a more leisurely dinner? Do some feed in groups while others dine alone?

BY A FIREFLY'S LIGHT

When oxygen combines with a chemical called luciferin, *bioluminescence* results. If you live east of the Rocky Mountains in North America, you've probably seen this chemical reaction. It produces the light of the firefly. Is the rate of this reaction related to the temperature of the environment? To find out, catch a firefly and put it in a small bottle or vial. Plug the opening of the vial with cotton or a porous material so that gases may pass to and from the vial. Lower the temperature by surrounding the bottle with ice cubes. Does the firefly's flash rate change? What happens to the flash rate if the firefly is placed in a warm environment?

Conduct a number of trials of this experiment. Carefully record both the flash rate and the temperature over a wide range of temperatures. Plot a graph of the results. Recording your results with a spreadsheet will allow easier graphing. A program like *Graphical Analysis* will allow you to easily try out various mathematical equations to see which one best fits the data. Do you find any mathematical relationship between flash rate and temperature?

Design an experiment to see how the concentration of oxygen affects the firefly's flash rate. Release the firefly when you are through experimenting.

THE CARE, FEEDING, AND STUDY OF MEALWORMS

You can observe the life cycle of an insect by watching mealworms (larvae of the darkling beetle).

Buy 100 to 200 larvae or pupae from a pet store or a biological supply house. Put them in a plastic, metal, or glass container that is at least 6 inches (15 cm) on a side. Cover the base of the container with a 2- to 3-inch (5- to 8-cm) layer of food—oatmeal, wheat bran, crushed dog biscuits, or chicken-laying mash. The animals can get their water from fruits and vegetables such as carrots, potatoes, or apples placed uncut on top of the food. Keep the food dry to avoid mold. Replace the pulpy fruits or vegetables whenever they dry out. Cover the container with a sheet of cardboard.

When the larvae form pupae, move the pupae to another container with a small amount of food. When the adult beetles emerge, return them to the original culture. If you leave a few pupae in the large container, you'll see why it's a good idea to remove the adults.

If you smell the pungent odor of ammonia or see mold on the food, it's time to move the animals to fresh food in another container. If the container becomes crowded with adults and larvae, move some animals to a new container. How long does it take these animals to go through a complete life cycle?

Mealworms (larvae) make interesting subjects for investigating animal behavior. Here are some questions that may serve as a framework for a series of experiments: Do mealworms prefer light or darkness? If they respond well to light, do they have a preference for a particular color? Does it make a difference if it is colored light or just colored backgrounds? How do mealworms respond to touch? Does it matter where you touch them? How do they respond to heat? To the odor of ammonia? To vinegar? Can you make a mealworm back up? Can they learn? Can they see?

SOW BUGS

One of the few crustaceans to successfully live on land is the sow bug, commonly called the pill bug or wood louse. You can find these isopods under stones and logs, where they feed on decaying vegetation. If you have trouble finding them, you may be able to attract some by leaving hollowed-out raw potatoes in moist, shaded areas.

You can culture sow bugs with a mixture of sand and peat moss in a coffee can or plastic container. Keep a moist sponge in their container and add a fresh piece of raw potato or carrot from time to time. Watch these animals for a few days and try to decide what conditions of temperature, light, and moisture they like best. After you have formulated your hypothesis, run some experimental tests.

Cover the bottom of a deep container with sand. Bury three petri dishes or large jar lids so that the top rims are level with the sand. Put some peat moss in each dish or lid. Soak the moss in one dish thoroughly, moisten the moss in the second dish, and leave the moss in the third dish completely dry. Cover half of each dish with a piece of black construction paper so that the moss under the paper is in darkness. Put a bright light above the container. Then place about a dozen sow bugs in the center of the container. Watch carefully. Where do the bugs finally come to rest? Were your hypotheses about light and moisture correct?

Design an experiment to test your hypothesis about the temperature the bugs prefer.

INSECTS IN THE DARK

The night air is often full of insect activity. You can attract and capture night insects with a light and a sheet. Insects will fly a "spiral" path around the light, and some of them will settle on a white sheet hung beside the light. How many settle on the sheet after 20 minutes? Examine those insects. What kinds do you find? Repeat the experiment for several nights. Does the number of insects you collect vary from night to night?

To trap the insects, secure a paper plate near a lightbulb. Then lay strips of sticky flypaper along the plate. What conditions seem to affect the nighttime insect population? Is it temperature? Wind? Humidity? Clouds?

Does the kind of insect flying about at night change with the seasons? For example, do you find June bugs only in June? What do you find when you try this experiment on nights with similar weather conditions, at different times of the spring, summer, and autumn?

Design an experiment to see whether the color of the light plays a role in attracting insects. Don't forget to try using "black light" (ultraviolet light).

COLLECTING SPIDER WEBS

Have you ever watched a spider spin a web? You'll find it fascinating—and you can preserve the web.

Use a can of white spray paint to paint the web lightly on both sides. Hold the can at least 24 inches (60 cm) from the web so that you don't damage the web. Start at the web's center and move outward. While the paint is still tacky, hold a heavy sheet of black construction paper gently against the web. With a fine brush, carefully break the points where the web is attached to its points of support.

After the paint dries, spray on several coats of clear varnish or cover the sheet with plastic wrap to preserve the web and seal it to the paper.

You can collect and compare the webs made by different

Although an orb spider spun this web to catch its dinner, we can enjoy its natural beauty.

species of spiders. Or you can watch one spider and examine the web it makes. Do the webs change as the spider ages? Some spiders decorate their webs. Can you find any webs with such decorations? Are these webs more effective at catching insects? Are they less effective?

If you have the patience to be a spider watcher, you'll find it worth your time. One student was able to get a project on a space shuttle to find out how spiders spin webs in zero gravity. How do spiders catch their food? How do they eat their prey? Do they gulp their food or do they enjoy a long dinner hour? How do spiders reproduce? If possible, place a sac of spider eggs in a jar and wait for them to hatch. Once the spiders hatch, release them or they'll eat each other. Watch several of them after they leave the jar. What do they do? Young spiders often disperse by a process called ballooning. What is ballooning? Try to observe it.

SWEEPING FOR INSECTS

Insects are most abundant in temperate and tropical climates. You can see this for yourself by sweeping for insects.

To make a sweeper, first find an insect net or make one from a cheesecloth bag, stiff wire, and an old broom handle. Then walk through an open field of tall grass and weeds. As you walk, swing the net back and forth through the grass and weeds. After you've swept your way across the field, grab the bag at the center and twist it several times to trap any insects you may have captured. Cover the net with a large plastic bag and tie the top of the bag to the handle of the net. Now untwist the net and turn it inside out to release the insects into the plastic bag.

How many insects did you catch? How many different species do you see? Can you identify them? What else do you find in the net?

Repeat this experiment at different times of the year. When are insects most abundant? Do you always catch the same kinds of insects, or do the species vary from month to month? Keep a record of your collection in a spreadsheet to make it easy to update, alphabetize, and print out specialized lists.

BREATHING FISH

You're right, fish don't breathe. But they do respire, just like all living things. When a fish gulps water, it doesn't swallow it. The water passes over the blood-vessel-rich tissue that makes up its gills. The gills are located under the flaps of skin that lie behind a fish's eyes. A fish gulping water is the equivalent of a mammal breathing. Both are taking oxygen into, and expelling carbon dioxide from, their blood. However, a fish is cold-blooded; its body temperature changes with the temperature of its environment.

Do you think the gulping rate of a fish changes as the water temperature changes? Will a fish's activity level affect its gulping rate? To find out, you'll need four goldfish, preferably Comet goldfish. Comets can withstand changes in water temperature quite well. You'll also need two tanks. Flat-sided tanks work best because they don't make the fish appear distorted the way round bowls do. Place two fish in each tank with water at 70°F (21°C). If you use chlorinated tap water, let it stand for several days before adding the fish.

When the fish seem quiet and used to your presence, count the gulping rate of each fish in gulps per minute. Make several counts and take an average. Then slowly raise the water temperature in one tank to 75°F (24°C) by adding and stirring in warm water. To avoid shocking the fish, it should take at least 20 minutes to make this temperature change. Similarly, and again very slowly, lower the temperature in the other tank to 65°F (18°C). After the temperatures in the two tanks are steady and the fish are quiet, record their gulping rates again.

Lower the temperature in the cooler tank, slowly as before, to 55°F (13°C). This should take at least 45 minutes. Raise the temperature in the other tank to 80°F (26°C). If the fish begin swimming to the surface as the water warms, stop adding warm water.

When these temperatures are achieved and the fish are quiet, measure their gulping rates again. What is the effect of temperature on the respiration rate in fish? How can you make goldfish more active? How does their activity level affect their gulping rate?

Does the size of the fish affect their respiration rate? How about the brightness of light around the tank? Does sound affect their respiration rate? Is classical music soothing to fish? Can you find other factors that affect a fish's respiration rate? Record your data for these trials in a spreadsheet and graph them. *Graphical Analysis* will allow you to try out various mathematical equations to see if any fit your data well.

How is the solubility of oxygen in water related to temperature? How is it related to your data? Why do many fish in some lakes and streams often die during hot summer months?

ANIMAL TRACKS

When animals walk in snow or soft dirt, they leave tracks. The tracks you see most often are those made by dogs or cats. Look carefully at tracks you know were made by a dog and a cat. How do the tracks compare? How many toes do these animals have? Does either animal leave toenail tracks? How do their walking patterns compare?

Is the size of an animal's track related to its height or weight? Measure these variables using available animals like neighbors' dogs and cats. Can you find more exotic animals at a zoo? Talk to a zookeeper. You may be able to obtain data on the animals' heights and weights as well as footprints.

Is there a mathematical relationship between an animal's tracks and its weight and height? Use *Graphical Analysis* to help you figure out a formula.

If you live in an area where it snows, take a walk in the woods after a light snowfall. Bring along a book that contains drawings or pictures of the footprints of common animals. How many different kinds of animals walked through the woods you visited? If it never snows in your area, try looking in sandy or dusty areas after wind has smoothed away old tracks, or near streams where animals drink.

You can preserve animal tracks in a variety of ways. One method is to photograph or draw pictures of the prints you see. It's a good idea to place a small ruler next to the animal's track so you can compare the relative sizes of the prints. You

The tracks in this photo tell us that a snowshoe hare has recently been here.

can cut silhouettes of the tracks from construction paper and paste them on white paper.

To make casts of footprints made in dirt, mix plaster of paris with water. When it has the right consistency, pour the plaster into the track until it flows over the sides. Wait 20 minutes for it to harden, then cut around the cast with a dull knife and lift it from the ground. Wash off the dirt and you will have a permanent record of the track.

To make a cast of a footprint left in snow, the temperature should be below freezing—32°F (0°C). Sprinkle a little water into the track. The water will freeze into a thin coat of ice over the track's surface, helping to prevent the weight of the plaster from spoiling the track. Mix some snow with the plaster to make it cold. Pour the plaster into the track very slowly to melt as little snow as possible.

You can also use melted paraffin to make casts of tracks, but you'll need a way to melt the wax. Of course, you could tip a burning candle and let melted wax flow into the track, but this method takes a long time.

You might also make casts with a liquid rubber compound. The resulting footprint can then be used to make more animal footprints with an ink pad.

APPENDIX 1

Science
Opportunities

Earthwatch
Offers research internships in various science projects throughout the world.
Earthwatch, 10 Juniper Road, Box 127, Belmont, MA 02178
(617) 489-3030

International Science and Engineering Fair
Sponsored by General Motors and almost fifty other organizations. Projects may be in any of twelve categories ranging from computers to zoology.
Science Service Inc., 1719 N Street NW, Washington, DC 20036-2890
(202) 785-2255 or http://www.tss-inc.com/sciserv/

Jackson Laboratory, Summer Student Program

Held every summer in Bar Harbor, Maine. Students work with staff members of the Jackson Laboratory who are engaged in bio-medical research.

Jackson Laboratory, Summer Student Program, 600 Main St. Bar Harbor, ME 04609-1500

(207) 288-3371 or

http://www.jax.org/training/documents/Summer.html

JETS

Holds a contest for projects in engineering.

Junior Engineering Technical Society, 345 East 47th Street, New York, NY 10017

http://www.asee.org/jets

National Science Foundation Science Training Project

Program sponsored by NSF that offers science training at many schools, colleges, and laboratories during the summer months.

Public Information Branch, National Science Foundation, Washington, DC 20550

http://www.nsta.org

NSTA/NASA Space Science Student Involvement Project

Gives students the opportunity to propose experiments to be done aboard the Space Shuttle. For grades 6–12.

National Science Teachers Association, NSTA/NASA Space Shuttle Student Involvement Project, 1742 Connecticut Avenue, NW, Washington, DC 20009

http://wwwedu.ssc.nasa.gov/htmls/ssc_stra.htm or //esther.la.asu.edu/asu/tes_Editor/CURRIC_GUIDES/94_9 5GUIDE/resource_nasa/html

Westinghouse Science Talent Search

Provides scholarships to winners of this program, which involves independent research in the physical, biological, behavioral, and social sciences, as well as in mathematics and engineering.

Science Service, 1719 N Street NW, Washington, DC 20036

http://www.tss-inc.com/sciserv/

APPENDIX 2

Statistics

"Statistics" is a word that you hear a lot these days. There are statistics that show that smoking causes lung cancer, statistics that show that wearing seat belts saves lives, and statistics showing that many people don't believe statistics.

Keep in mind that you should always use caution when you read a conclusion based on statistics. For example, in a newspaper article touting the virtues of a high-fiber diet (one with lots of raw vegetables and bran and very little meat or fat), a comparison was made between the health of people in the United States and the health of people in one part of Africa.

According to the statistics, people on a high-fiber diet in that part of Africa had a much smaller chance of dying from heart disease than did residents of the United States. The conclusion drawn from these statistics was that the large amount of fiber in the African diets "protected" these people from heart disease.

However, even though those conclusions could be made from that set of data, let's take a closer look at the sample populations—the populations that were studied. When the sample included only those people over age 55, it turned out that the trend was reversed. People over 55 in that part of Africa had a much greater chance of dying of heart disease than did people in the same age group in the United States.

The people in Africa had a high risk of dying of conditions such as cholera, typhoid, tuberculosis, malaria, or malnutrition long before they reached age 55. In the United States, very few people die from those things today, so many more live long enough to develop the degenerative disorders such as heart disease and cancer.

WHY USE STATISTICS?

If statistics cause so much confusion, why are they used in science?

Because scientists can be lazy.

Perhaps you can identify with that. Suppose you're trying to get some of the "stats" on the middle-school football team and you have the weights of the linemen and their substitutes: 185, 230, 130, 178, 267, 137, 187, 177, 201, and 212 pounds. There are only ten numbers, but even ten three-digit numbers are hard to remember. One easy way to get a general idea of the team members' weights would be to calculate the average. Add up all ten weights and divide by the number of players: 1,904 ÷ 10 = 190 lbs. (190.4 rounded off) to get the weight of the average player.

"AVERAGE" VERSUS "NORMAL"

Does this mean that a normal football lineman on the middle-school team weighs 190 pounds? Not really, because average and normal are not the same thing. Think about the projection that the "average family" in the United States will soon have 1.3 children. Will there be any average families in the United States? Probably not. On the other hand, a normal family could have three, two, one, or even no children at all.

How do you determine what's normal when you're dealing with something totally new? You could use statistics.

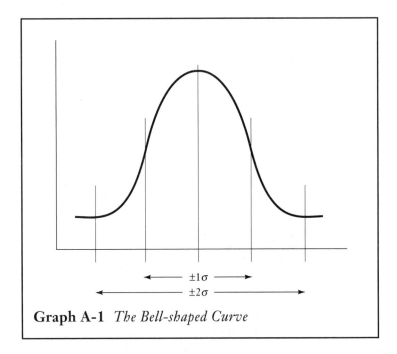

Graph A-1 *The Bell-shaped Curve*

First, let's consider what "normal" means. Take a look at Graph A-1. This graph has been called a bell-shaped curve or "bell curve," because the curve looks something like a bell. (We'll get to the "1σ" and "2σ" later.)

The height of the graph indicates the number of observations of a given variable along a scale that stretches across the bottom (or horizontal axis) of the graph. For example, we could plot the heights of all adults on this graph, with the height of the shortest person on the far left and the height of the tallest on the far right. Most people would fall somewhere in the large center area of the graph, which then would represent the majority of people, or what could be considered "normal." Far fewer people would fall in either "tail" of the curve, representing those people who are either very short or very tall.

How can the heights of all adults graph to such a nice curve? That's hard to answer, but many different kinds of observations seem to fit that curve. We could put people's shoe sizes on the curve, or their intelligence, scores on a test (that's the famous "grading on the curve"), populations of bacteria, and so on.

The fact that so many things fit this curve helps us to determine what's normal. In a bell curve, the observations that fall between the two lines marked by ± 1σ represent 68 percent of all the observations, and are usually considered "normal."

AVERAGE AND "AVERAGE DIFFERENCE"

Let's go back to the numbers representing the weights of the football players. We calculated the average weight of the players by dividing the total weight of all the players by the number of players to get 190.4 pounds. Then we can ask, "How much does each player's weight differ from the average," since nobody's weight exactly equals the average. Let's set up Table A-1. This is easy to do on a computer spreadsheet (see the Appendix 3).

With this information, we can calculate the average difference—how much each player's weight differs from the average.

If you add the numbers in the last column, you get a total of zero. Instead, ignore any negative signs and then add the numbers. The sum of the differences is 296.8. Divide that number by the total number of players, 10, to get the average difference: 29.68. But remember, we ignored the positive and negative signs in our calculations, so we should call the average difference "plus or minus 29.68 pounds."

TABLE A-1   INFORMATION FOR A SPREADSHEET

Player	Weight (lbs.)	Average (lbs.)	[Weight] – [Average] Difference from Average
1	185	190.4	−5.4
2	230	190.4	39.6
3	130	190.4	−60.4
4	178	190.4	−12.4
5	267	190.4	76.6
6	137	190.4	−53.4
7	187	190.4	−3.4
8	177	190.4	−13.4
9	201	190.4	10.6
10	212	190.4	21.6

Now we can say that the average player weighs 190.4 pounds, plus or minus 29.68 pounds (written by scientists as 190.4 ± 29.68). No player weighs exactly 190.4 pounds, but most of them fall into the range of about 160 to 220 pounds.

VARIANCE AND STANDARD DEVIATION

Figuring out the average difference in this way is reasonable, and the answers we get seem to make sense. How is this different from the method statisticians use?

Remember before when we ignored the plus and minus signs? Another way to do this is to multiply each number by itself—square it. You probably know that multiplying a negative number by another negative number results in a positive number. Of course, multiplying two positive numbers also gives a positive result. In this way, we can get rid of all the negatives.

Look at Table A-2. The sum of the squared differences gives a total of 14,888.4, or an average of 1488.84. This is called the *variance*. Of course, for our purposes, to get a number that's easier to understand, we have to undo all that squaring we did. Finding the

TABLE A-2   INFORMATION FOR A SPREADSHEET

Player	Weight (lbs.)	Average (lbs.)	[Weight] – [Average] Difference from Average (lbs.)	[Difference]²
1	185	190.4	−5.4	29.16
2	230	190.4	39.6	1568.16
3	130	190.4	−60.4	3648.16
4	178	190.4	−12.4	153.76
5	267	190.4	76.6	5867.56
6	137	190.4	−53.4	2851.56
7	187	190.4	−3.4	11.56
8	177	190.4	−13.4	179.56
9	201	190.4	10.6	112.36
10	212	190.4	21.6	466.56

square root is easy with a calculator or a computer. The square root of 14,888.4 is 38.59. This is called the *standard deviation*.

The neat thing about the standard deviation is that with a large sample, the center area on a bell curve—the part that contains the majority of the observations—will be within one standard deviation above or below the average. This is written as "1 std.dev." or "1σ" from the Greek letter sigma (σ). If you mark everything that is plus or minus one standard deviation from the average, you should get 68 percent of all the observations. If you go two standard deviations to either side of the average (±2σ), you'll include 95 percent of the observations. Using the standard deviation can tell you where the tails of the curve should be, without having to graph all your information. If a value falls outside of the central area, you know it's pretty unusual and deserves more study. If something looks different but falls within the standard deviation, it's just part of normal variability and isn't different enough to count; it's not statistically significant.

For example, you could do a plant experiment in which you compare variable sunlight versus indoor light on the growth rates of the plants. You could also change the type of indoor light by using fluorescent or regular tungsten (incandescent) lightbulbs. You might even wish to vary the type of fluorescent tubes: the standard cool white, full-spectrum bulbs, or even the purplish "grow lights."

In all these cases, the plants will exhibit different rates of growth. But then, plants in any group will exhibit different growth rates—any gardener will tell you that. You can use standard deviation to tell what's statistically "normal" and what is a truly significant difference in growth rates.

Using statistics to understand your data not only makes it easier for you to tell what's significant, it also looks impressive to science teachers and science fair judges. If you want to learn more about statistics, there are many statistics books of varying complexity and usefulness. Talking to your math teacher can help too. Also, programs such as *Graphical Analysis* from Vernier Software will help you with correlation tests.

APPENDIX 3

Spreadsheets and Graphics

Back in the early days of the microcomputer—about 1978—two people developed a program called *VisiCalc*. This was the first successful spreadsheet program; it mimicked something the business community had been using for years. Before computers, spreadsheets were big sheets of paper, marked off in a grid perfect for displaying information. For example, on one sheet department stores recorded all the sales by departments in one column. The data for each day of the week was recorded in parallel columns on the grid. At the end of the week, adding up the numbers across each row would give the sales for each department for the whole week. Adding the numbers in one column would give the total sales for all departments for a given day.

From there, a manager could do more calculations to get other useful figures, such as sales per square foot of space for each department, or cost of salaries per sale. The information was great for planning, but the calculations involved were tedious. Then came the computer spreadsheet, and the industry really took off.

Scientists and science students can use computer spreadsheets to make calculations and graphs. Recall the example from the middle-school football team used in Appendix 2. Table A-3 is similar to Table A-2, but with a little modification.

TABLE A-3   INFORMATION FOR A SPREADSHEET

	A	B	C	D	E
1	Player	Weight	Average	Difference	Diff^2
2	1	185	190.4	−5.4	29.16
3	2	230	190.4	39.6	1568.16
4	3	130	190.4	−60.4	3648.16
5	4	178	190.4	−12.4	153.76
6	5	267	190.4	76.6	5867.56
7	6	137	190.4	−53.4	2851.56
8	7	187	190.4	−3.4	11.56
9	8	177	190.4	−13.4	179.56
10	9	201	190.4	10.6	112.36
11	10	212	190.4	21.6	466.56

Notice how each row is labeled with a number, and each column with a letter. We could refer to the weight of Player 5 as "B6," the number at the intersection of column B and row 6.

The calculations in this table weren't done by hand. They were done using a computer spreadsheet. Once we entered the weights of the players in column B, the computer calculated the rest of the numbers. We simply had to tell it how to perform each calculation. For example, we "clicked" on cell D2, and told the computer that the difference is calculated by subtracting the average weight of all the players from a player's weight; that is, when we clicked on D2, we typed "=B2 − C2." When we clicked on cell E2, we typed "=D2*D2". This told the computer to calculate the numbers in column E by multiplying the number in column D with itself.

You can probably find a computer spreadsheet at home or at school. Many "all-in-one" programs, such as *ClarisWorks*, *Microsoft Works*, *WordPerfect Works*, *GreatWorks*, or others, have a spreadsheet module built in. Sometimes a spreadsheet such as Excel is linked to another set of programs so that each program can "talk" to the others. That's the way *Microsoft Office* and *WordPerfect Office* work. You can do all the calculations you need and copy the resulting table into a word-processing document.

Most spreadsheet programs include a graphing program or module. Separate graphing programs will offer you more flexibility and more types of graphs. Usually, for the all-in-one programs, you highlight a section of your spreadsheet, choose a graph type, and the graphing module makes the graph for you.

Even though the hard part is done for you, you'll need to make sure that you've chosen a graph type suitable for your data and intended audience.

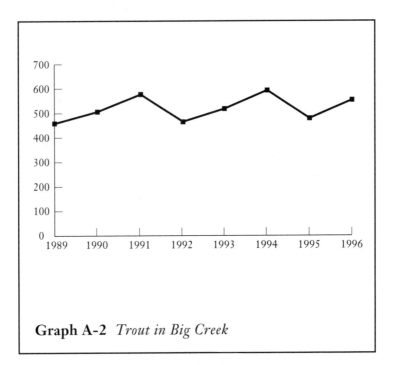

Graph A-2 *Trout in Big Creek*

Graph A-2 shows the population of a particular species of fish in an area, Big Creek, over several years. We supplied the data in Table A-4, and let the computer choose its own format.

TABLE A-4   BIG CREEK TROUT POPULATION

Year	Trout
1989	458
1990	510
1991	580
1992	470
1993	520
1994	600
1995	490
1996	560

Looking at Graph A-2, it appears that the trout population in the creek is about equal from year to year. But if we tell the graphing program to use 450 as its lowest value and 600 as the highest, the graph looks very different. See Graph A-3. Choosing a range for the graph that's closer to the range of the data makes the changes in the trout population look much more extreme.

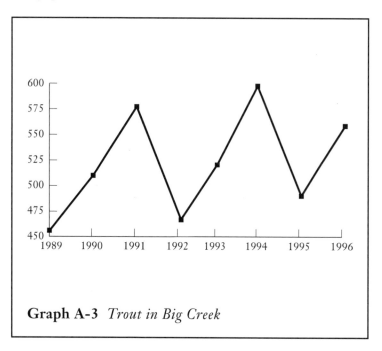

Graph A-3 *Trout in Big Creek*

How you present your data can be as important to your science project as the data itself. Was your purpose in doing this fish count to show that Big Creek has had a stable population over the years you studied? Or was your purpose to show that Big Creek suffers from drastic fish kills every 3 years? Choose your graph accordingly.

If you use a special graphing program, such as *DeltaGraph 4.0* you can get fancy, three-dimensional graphs. They may look impressive in science fairs, but do they show what you want them to?

What about bar graphs, pie charts, or histograms? You need to make decisions about what to graph, and how to graph it. What exactly do you want to show?

GLOSSARY

absolute humidity—the mass of water that can dissolve in 1 cubic meter of air.

accelerate—to undergo a change in velocity.

bioluminescence—the light emitted by living organisms.

bob (of a pendulum)—the weight that swings back and forth.

cotyledon—the first leaf that developes from a spouting seed.

conductor—a material through which electricity and/or heat flows easily.

critical mass—the amount of matter great enough to cause a change.

density—mass per unit volume.

dewpoint—the temperature at which moisture begins to condense from the air.

efficiency—the ratio of amount of energy or work put out to the amount of energy or work put in.

focal length—the distance of a focus from the center of a lens or mirror.

friction—a force that resists the motion between two objects or surfaces. If there is motion, energy is converted to heat.

horsepower—a unit of power equal to 746 watts or 550 foot•pounds/second.

insulator—a material that does not conduct electricity and/or heat easily.

joule—a unit of work or energy equal to the work done by 1 newton acting through a distance of 1 meter.

Lugol's solution—a solution of iodine and potassium iodide crystals in water.

microclimate—the climate of a small system.

ohm—a unit of electrical resistance equal to the resistance of a circuit in which a potential difference of 1 volt produces a current of 1 ampere.

period (of a pendulum)—the time it takes for a pendulum to complete one full swing.

photosynthesis—the food-making process of green plants.

power—the rate at which work is done.

principal focus—the point where parallel light rays that have been reflected or refracted meet.

real image—an image that has been "captured' on a screen because the rays of light from an object are brought together at a series of points corresponding to the points on the object from which they came.

reflect—to bend aside or turning back ight. Light may be reflected by a mirror or a piece of white paper.

refract—to bend light as it enters or exits a transparent substance, such as glass.

relative humidity—the ratio of absolute humidity to the maximum amount of water vapor that the air could hold per cubic meter if it were saturated.

standard deviation—in statistics, an average difference from the average that will contain 68 percent of all the data in a random sample.

thermocouple probe—a instrument used to measure very slight changes in temperature precisely.

variance—in statistics, the sum of the square of the standard deviation.

virtual image—an image formed by diverging light rays that appear to be coming from a series of points located, for example, behind a plane mirror.

work—force multipled by the distance through which the force acts.

FOR FURTHER READING

Ardley, Neil. *101 Great Science Experiments*. New York: Dorling Kindersley, 1993.

Barr, George. *Science Research Experiments for Young People*. New York: Dover Publications, 1989.

Bochinski, Julianne Blair. *The Complete Handbook of Science Fair Projects*. New York: Wiley, 1996.

Collins, Kevin and Betty Collins. *Experimenting with Science Photography*. New York: Franklin Watts, 1994.

Gardner, Robert. *Robert Gardner's Favorite Science Experiments*. New York: Franklin Watts, 1992.

Gardner, Robert. *Robert Gardner's Challenging Science Experiments*. New York: Franklin Watts, 1993.

Krieger, Melanie Jacobs. *How to Excel in Science Competitions*. New York: Franklin Watts, 1991.

Krieger, Melanie Jacobs. *Means and Probabilities: Using Statistics in Science Projects*. New York: Franklin Watts, 1996.

Markle, Sandra. *The Young Scientist's Guide to Successful Science Projects*. New York: Lothrop, Lee and Shepard, 1990.

Newton, David E. *Making and Using Scientific Equipment*. New York: Franklin Watts, 1993.

O'Neil, Karen E. *Health and Medicine Projects for Young Scientists*. New York: Franklin Watts, 1993.

Provenzo, Eugene F. and Asterie Baker Provenzo. *47 Easy-To-Do Classic Science Experiments*. New York: Dover Publications, 1989.

Rybolt, Thomas. *Environmental Experiments about Renewable Energy*. Springfield, NJ: Enslow Publishers, 1994.

Tocci, Salvatore. *How to Do a Science Fair Project, Revised Edition*. Danbury, CT: Franklin Watts, 1997.

INTERNET RESOURCES

Due to the changeable nature of the Internet, sites appear and disappear very quickly. These resources offered useful information on science projects at the time of publication.

Science Sites with "Links" to Many Other Places

Address	Site
http://www.exploratorium.edu/	Exploratorium Home Page
http://www.npr.org/~scifri	NPR's Science Friday Kids' Connection
http://nyelabs.kcts.org	Bill Nye the Science Guy
http://www.stemnet.nf.ca/~jbarron/scifair.html	Science Fair Home Page
http://ericir.syr.edu/Projects/Newton/tryit.html	PBS's Newton's Apple "Science Try-its"
http://www.scri.fus.edu/~dennisl/special/sf_helpers.html	Ask Science Fair Questions
http://www.isd77.k12.mn.us/resources/cf/SciProjIntro.html	Guide to doing science projects
http://www.waterw.com/~sciencel/kids.htm	Curious Kids Science Newsletter
http://www.yahoo.com/Education/Math_and_Science_Education/Fairs/	Guide to science fairs worldwide

General Science Project Information

Address	Site
http://www.tc.cornell.edu/Visualization/animations/animations.html	Scientific images and animations
http://www.calpoly.edu/delta.html	Biological sciences database
http://muse.bio.cornell.edu/11/images	Biology image archive

http://mentor.external.hp.com	HP e-mail science mentors
http://unite2.tisl.ukans.edu/	Thousands of lessons in science
http://www.eskimo.com/~billb/amateur/saslgosm.gif	Society of Amateur Science demos
http://www.hmco.com/hmco.com/hmco/school/links/ask.html	Ask an expert
http://www.energy.ca.gov/energy/education/projects-html/projects.html	Energyquest Energy Projects

Chapter 1

Address	Site
http://www.dwatcm.wr.usgs.gov/askhyd.html	Ask a hydrologist
http://walrus.wr.usgs.gov/docs/ask-a-ge.html	Ask a geologist
http://www.weather.com/metnet.html	Ask a meteorologist
http://crusher.bev.net/education/SeaWorld/ask_shamu/asintro.html	Ask an oceanographer

Chapters 2 and 3

Address	Site
http://www.halcyon.com/rupe/atmj/	Amateur telescope makers' journal
http://northshore.shore.net/~toddg/welcome.htm	Weather/astronomy page
http://www2.ari.net/home/odenwald/qadir/qanda.html	Ask an astronomer
http://www.opticalres.com/kidoptx.html	Optics for kids
http://www.eskimo.com/~billb/amateur/teles.txt	Quick and simple telescope

http://www.eskimo.com/ ~billb/tesla.heli1.txt	How to build a plasma globe
http://www.achilles.net/~jtalbot/ amateur/index.html	Natural lasers
http://www.uq.oz.au/nanoworld/ nanohome.html	Excellent source for electron microscope images
http://www.exploratorium.edu/ publications/Snackbook/ Snackbook.html	Projects dealing with all sorts of physical science and optical illusions

Chapter 4

Address	Site
http://xenon.chem.uidaho.edu/labs/ ICE/concepts1.html	Fun with Chemistry ONE
http://xenon.chem.uidaho.edu/labs/ ICE/concepts2.html	Fun with Chemistry TWO
http://www.chem.lsu.edu/form.html	Ask a chemist
http://www.math.ucla.edu/~barry/ CF/suppliers.html	Chemical suppliers' list
http://www.nyu.edu/mathmol/	Molecular modeling
http://esg-www.mit.edu:8001/ esgbio/eb/ebdir.html	Enzymes
http://molbio.info.nih.gov/ cgi-bin/pdb	Molecules R Us Protein data bank
http://www.scimedia.com/chem-ed/ scidex.htm	Hypermedia index to chemistry methods, instruments, and software

Chapter 5

Address	Site
http://192.239.146.18/PSAM.html	Physical Science Activity Manual
http://129.82.166.181/default.html	Little Shop of Physics
http://129.82.166.181/ Experiments.html	Physics experiments

http://nike.phy.bris.ac.uk:8080/ dr_neutrino/ask.html	Ask Dr. Neutrino
http://alcom.kent.edu/ALCOM/ K12/ASK/Ask_feedback.html	Ask about physics
http://www2.ncsu.edu:80/ncsu/ pams/ physics/Edu_Resources/ demoroom/demoroom.html	Physics demos
http://www.physics.mcgill.ca/ physics-services/	Physics around the world interactive

Chapter 6

Address	Site
http://www.eskimo.com/~billb/ amateur/mirror.html	How to build a solar furnace
http://www.eskimo.com/~billb/ amateur/lavalamp.txt	How to build a lava lamp
http://njnie.dl.stevens-tech.edu/ curriculum/science.html	Science/math/technology experts
http://volcano.und.nodak.edu. vwdocs/ask_a.html	Ask a volcanologist

Chapter 7

Address	Site
http://www.eskimo.com/~billb/ emotor/stick.html	Electrostatics
http://www.eskimo.com/~billb/ emotor/vdg.html	Van de Graaff generator
http://www.eskimo.com/~billb/ amateur/coilgen.html	Simple electric generator
http://www.eskimo.com/~billb/ emotor/emotor.html	Motor from plastic soda bottles
http://www.eskimo.com/~billb/ emotor/electoph.txt	Electrostatic generator
http://www.eskimo.com/~billb/ electrom/electrom.html	See electrostatic fields

Address	Site
http://www.eskimo.com/~billb/ viselect/viselect.html	Make electricity visible in wires
http://home.earthlink.net/~lenyr/	Spark, Bang, Buzz
http://schoolnet2.carleton.ca/ english/math_sci/phys/electric-club/	The Electric Club projects
http://www.york.ac.uk/~mjgw100/ esl/eslhowto.htm	Make electrostatic loud speakers
http://fly.hiwaar.net/~palmer/ motor.html	Beakman Motor project
http://www.eskimo.com/~billb/ suppliers.html	Suppliers of electronics

Chapter 8

Address	Site
http://www.atlcard.com/ ask_md.html	Ask a cardiologist
http://www.dentistinfo.com/ aska.htm	Ask a dentist
http://www.hoptechno.com/ rdindex.htm	Ask a dietician
http://www.neoucom.edu?DEPTS/ NEUR/WEB/neuromail.html	Ask a neurobiologist
http://weber.u.washington.edu/ ~chudler/neurok.html	Neuroscience for kids
http://www1.biostr.washington.edu/ DigitalAnatomist.html	Interactive 3-D images of brain
http://www.virginia.edu/~biotimin/ TUTORIALMAIN.html	Human clock/sleep-wake cycles
http://www.socsci.uci.edu/cogsci/ projects/civs/civs.html	Color in visual search
http://www.cpmc.columbia.edu/ homepages/morrowj/tools/bsa.html	Body surface area calculator
http://www.cs.brown.edu/people/oa/ Bin/skeleton.html	Clickable human skeleton

Chapter 9

Address	Site
http://www.grower-2-you.com/expert.html	Ask a horticulturist
http://newcrop.hort.purdue.edu/	Crops of the U.S. index
http://www.helsinki.fi/kmus/botgard.html	Links to worldwide gardens
http://ampere.scale.uiuc.edu/~m-lexa/cell.html	Images, texts, movies of plant cells
http://155.187.10.12/anbg.html	Australian botanical gardens
http://www.hpl.hp.com/bot/cp_home	Carnivorous plant database
http://aquat1.ifas.ufl.edu/	Center for aquatic and ancient plants
http://ifs.plants.ox.ac.uk/wwd/pweeds.htm	World weeds database
http://fedwww.gsfc.nasa.gov/	Forest ecosystem dynamics

Chapter 10

Address	Site
http://www.ics.uci.edu/~pazzani/4H/InfoDirtRoad.html	4-H Farm
http://netvet.wustl.edu.htm	Electronic zoo of animals
http://george.ibl.gov/ITG.hm.pg.docs/Whole.Frog/Whole.Frog.html	3-D whole frog body visuals
http://curry.edschool.Virginia.EDU:80/~insttech/frog/	Interactive frog dissection
http://dns.ufsia.ac.be/Arachnology/Arachnology.html	Spiders and scorpions
http://www.actwin.com/WWWVL-Fish.html	Aqariums, ichthyology
http://www.ex.ac.uk/~gjlramel/welcome.html	Bug Club

http://www.life.uiuc.edu/Entomology/insectgifs.html	Insect drawings
http://bluehen.ags.udel.edu/insects/descriptions/entohome.html	On-line insect database
http://www.ent.iastate.edu/imagegallery.html	Insect Images
http://www.bev.net/education/SeaWorld/teacherguides.html	Whales and dolphins
http://www.aaa.com.au/A_Z/index.html	Australian animals
http://www.embl-heidelberg.de/~uetz/Reptiles.html	Links to reptile information sources

Besides the Web sites you can visit for information, you may need to find equipment and resources your school isn't able to supply. You can do an Internet search to find what you need. Here are some suggestions, including places with surplus and really cheap things:

Science Education Suppliers/Stores

Address	Site
http://cybershopping.com/eureka/handson.html	Hands-on science education products
http://nctweb.com/nct/value/edu.html	Value-Ware Science Education software
http://www.4free.com/homeschool/science.htm	Homeschool Store, Science
http://www.sycamoretree.com/scigen.html	Sycamore Tree catalog, science
http://www.lynxmotion.com	Lynxmotion Robot Kit
http://www.nadasci.com/catpage.htm	NDA Scientific, education devices
http://www.pasco.com	PASCO science education supplies
http://www.sciencekits.com	Rockville Creative Learning
http://www.carosci.com/carosci/	Carolina Biological Supply

http://www.eskimo.com/~billb/ supliers.html#edmund	Edmund Scientific
http://www.sargentwelch.com	Sargent-Welch catalog
http://branch.com/arbor/arbor.html	Arbor Scientific's catalog of science demos, toys
http://scitech.lm.com	SCITECH science store
http://www.service.com/stv/ home.html	Science Television
http://branch.com/infovid/ infovid.html	InfoVid Outlet: The Educational & How-To Video Warehouse

Surplus and Parts Suppliers

Address	Site
http://www.eskimo.com/~billb/ supliers.html	Surplus mail-order catalogs for science/electronics hobbyists
http://www.math.ucla.edu/~barry/ CF/suppliers.html	Chemical Suppliers list
http://www.sciplus.com	American Science & Surplus (formerly Jerryco)
http://www.pweb.com/mwk/main. htm	MWK Surplus Lasers & Optics
http://www.lasermotion.com/ catindx.html	Lasermotion Catalog
http://www.crl.com/~mdscienc	MD SCIENCE
http://www.ulysses.net/medused	Scientific Equipment Liquidators
http://www.cts.com/browse/rcivi Exchange	Scientific Equipment
http://www.johnstone.com	Surplus equipment
http://www.westes.com/site	Electronics equipment swap site

INDEX